# FOREVER
## AND FOR ALL TO SEE

**How to Avoid a** Social Media Scandal

**AND**

**How to Survive One**

AWARD-WINNING JOURNALIST
# CATHERINE BOSLEY
WITH IAN CORZINE, YOUR SOCIAL MEDIA LAWYER

CATHERINE BOSLEY

ISBN 979-8-98507-31-0-2 (paperback)

www.CatherineBosley.com

Dedicated to my dear mom and husband.
Thank you for all your patience, support, and the love
to power me through *everything* I do.

# ACKNOWLEDGEMENTS

On the personal side, I count my blessings every day to have the family and friends I have—the people who are my world. None of my work would mean anything if it weren't for my army. I thank God for surrounding me with such wonderful people, and, of course, for all He does to guide me. Dedicating this book to my husband, Rick, and my mom, Alice, still doesn't come close to expressing just how very precious they are to me. You two have been with me every step of the way on this project, seeing me through it with incredible patience. I'm also so grateful for support from the best brother anyone could have, and one of the kindest people I know, my brother, Jack, my wonderful dad, Ron, and precious stepdaughters, Laura and Jen, as well as my new sister-in-law, Dianna. A small but mighty family when it comes to supplying the kind of love and support needed to make dreams come true.

To the friends who've also seen me through the many steps of this project, I can't tell you how much I appreciate your belief in me. Jeanne, Michele, Tricia and Karen—I just love you ladies. And my dear friend (not to mention, best attorney ever), Andy Kabat, if it weren't for you, I don't know where I'd be. A true hero.

Also, cheers to my newer friends who I feel like I've known for years, Yolanda Albergottie, Lisa Ryan and John DiJulius. Your inspiration and encouragement are truly what made me sit down and finally begin this project I'd put off far too long.

On the professional side, I've also been truly blessed with such talented, and most importantly, caring collaborators. It starts with David Gray, of Gray Publishing in Cleveland, opening my eyes to the possibility of this book in the first place. Your guidance and consultation along the way have been invaluable. Editor, Eve Porinchak, in Los Angeles. You've gone above and beyond in helping polish these pages to a level far beyond what I expected. I can't wait until the day we meet in person and I can give you a big hug (and until we begin work for my next book, THE BARE FACTS).

Ian Corzine, you are amazing at your craft and great to work with, I so appreciate your contributions. My appreciation also goes out to my book designer, Brent Spears—amazing work and know-how. And I'd like to give a big shout out to my web designers, Sam and Anna Natello, of Dotcom Global Media. To my speaking agent, Melissa Beer of Rebelle Events, I'm grateful for every stage you get me on, but mostly for your kindness and the wisdom beyond your years that you generously share.

Finally, to all the high school and college educators, and business and association leaders who hired me over the last few years to speak to their groups, my deepest appreciation for the opportunity and for the trust bestowed upon me. It's that time I spent with your groups, and the incredible response I received from them (and you) that took my belief in my own mission and message to the next level.

# TO THE READER

Thank you for opening this book. I hope it lives up to your expectations. We all know nothing is perfect, but in my attempt to get FOREVER AND FOR ALL TO SEE as close to that as possible, I'm planning future editions, with some additions, deletions, and other modifications. I welcome you to contribute. If you feel I need to expand or pull back in certain sections, for instance, I'd like your input to consider for the next edition. If you have your own story to share that might strengthen a particular area it would be great to hear from you! You can email me at Catherine@CatherineBosley.com, or reach me through any of the major social media platforms: Facebook, Twitter, Instagram, LinkedIn. I also invite you to follow me on any of those platforms for the latest information regarding this book, how we can work together or how I can help you.

I also want you to know I did alter some of the information in some of the stories in these pages, including names, solely to protect those involved. That would include a few people who trusted me with their stories, whose trust I wouldn't want to betray. As this book highlights the need to respect each other's privacy, I felt modifications were necessary to do just that in those situations in this book that weren't otherwise already widely publicized.

Please watch for my next book, THE BARE FACTS. It is my memoir—the foundation of this book. You'll see I do include significant parts of my story in the following chapters to help you understand my fascination and growing knowledge on the topic of better navigating our day of digital everything. THE BARE FACTS is much different in that it digs into the very surreal story much deeper and provides insight on this topic from a more personal and emotional perspective. I can't wait to let you know when it's released.

Again, my thanks to you! Enjoy your read.

# FOREWORD

I had the pleasure of meeting Catherine Bosley through a mutual friend. Because I've been a professional speaker since 2010, he thought that I may be able to help Catherine with her burgeoning speaking career. My first thought was, "I don't do speaker training or coaching. I'm not sure how I can help her." But I said I'd see what I could do. I decided to check her out before our conversation so I could get an idea of her "story." That took me right to her TEDx Talk, and I was an immediate fan.

Soon after, we met for breakfast and I got to know her on a personal level. Catherine is kind, brilliant, and utterly captivating in her ability to tell a very difficult story and share the lessons she learned along the way. Catherine's tale is as compelling as it is precautionary. She knows exactly how to make you think about navigating today's online world from a different perspective.

I often joke with my friends that I'm so glad that social media was NOT around in my formative years. I never had to worry about being turned down for a job, being harassed about my looks, or getting "flamed" due to something I posted on social media. Theoretically, I don't have to worry about the things I did or said decades ago coming back to haunt me. Whew! However, Catherine's experience happened just as our digital world was taking shape and before we had any idea how pervasive and invasive it would become, especially with the onslaught of social media in our daily lives.

Since I began using social media, I've become aware of the long-term ramifications of what I post there. Catherine's story is the perfect example—a spur of the moment decision that nearly cost her everything, literally. Unfortunately, I see many of my friends, colleagues, and relatives posting things that have the potential to do lots of future damage. And no matter how quickly they hit "delete," that post never really goes away.

That's why what Catherine has to say in this book is so important to read and to share. Anyone who posts on social media will find priceless value in these pages as she translates her life-changing experience into unique enlightenment for the rest of us. The lessons learned here can save you, your friends, your kids, your colleagues—anyone you care about—from embarrassment, heartache, job loss, or even not getting a job in the first place.

Knowing how passionate Catherine is about her mission to use her story and insight to help others through her speaking events, I'm so glad she's decided to unpack it in a book as well—in order to reach even more people. You will be, too. This isn't your traditional "how to" book,  as it also serves as a great resource to keep handy.

What Catherine is doing with the hard lessons she's learned takes a level of vulnerability that not many people have—continuously talking about and revisiting something so painful and raw. Her idea of "FOREVER AND FOR ALL TO SEE," will change the reader—for the good—and will help prevent future online personal and professional catastrophes from happening.

Lisa Ryan
Speaker/Author
Chief Appreciation Strategist at Grategy

# CONTENTS

# INTRODUCTION

## WHO AM I TO TELL YOU? GREAT QUESTION.

"You're such a prissy little bitch, your days are over. Have a very Merry Christmas." Words that shook my soul. That was the end of the 30-second-long phone message I retrieved on Christmas morning 2003 that would set my nightmare, my scandal, into motion. Even all these years later, every time I hear that recording my heart sinks a bit and, for a moment, I hate myself all over again.

Still, I play the entire recording at every one of my speaking events, from high schools to corporate events. Why? It works. It's an attention-grabbing preamble to the two-fold cautionary, yet inspirational, message I have for people like you, who have hopes and dreams that deserve to be protected. While I'm still inclined to hide my face as the phone recording plays out to my audiences, it only took a a handful of responses following my first few events to let me know I NEED to do this:

From a high school teacher:

> *"**You saved someone's life today.** You showed these kids that it is possible to survive and succeed after going through something like this. Thank you so much!!"*

From a Facebook follower:

> *"My 13-year-old daughter has been relentlessly bullied both at school and online and somehow hearing your situation has **eased her hopelessness** for the time being. Thank you, my kind friend, for sharing your story and making my little girl feel a little better about herself. I am eternally grateful."*

The woman who left that phone message didn't leave her name, or any clue who she was. But the venom in her voice was enough to make it clear I was in real trouble. I nearly fell to my knees. The Christmas music playing in the background faded away. A heat came over my entire body as I stood in the kitchen with the phone to my ear, watching my husband and stepdaughters dance around and laugh, while working on our Christmas feast. We were expecting a houseful of guests.

Until that phone call, I had no idea pictures and video from a harmless but irresponsible vacation night with my husband, not even a year earlier, had gone viral. That decision I made that night, which ended up out there for the world to see, cost me my dream job as a TV news anchor at the time. I was let go. It cost me some friends, and any sense of self-respect. The humiliation from the fallout almost cost me my life, at my own hands.

It was a *what was I thinking* moment of stepping out of character and cutting loose in a way I never imagined I could, but in a way so many people still do today. Especially in a place like Key West, Florida. Especially during a time like spring break. What happened there was meant for the moment and, not too long ago, it could've stayed in the past with a lesson learned. It would've never resurfaced like it did, and on Christmas morning of all days. Today, the grim reality is that nothing meant for the moment is guaranteed to stay there. There is so little room for a lapse of judgement before that unfortunate episode could become attached to you *forever and for all to see*, one mouse click away, and erupt into life-changing scandal.

In my case, not only did my "mistake" go viral, but I was inundated with requests for interviews from the media—my own people—not just from around the country, but around the world. All of them with that question, "What were you thinking?" The phone would not stop ringing—*Good Morning America, Inside Edition, Oprah, The O'Reilly Factor*, to name a few. When I agreed to give an interview or appear on a show, my intention was to apologize, to try to explain my mindset that unfortunate night, and, most importantly, raise awareness about how our digital reality is rapidly encroaching on our privacy. But every time I agreed to an interview, things got worse. I became shamefully infamous. My name topped major search engine lists, above A-listers at the time like Brittany Spears and Paris Hilton.

Aside from knowing my own stupidity was to blame, what was happening online was the worst part. Hundreds of comments poured in every day from strangers. Some saying I was stupid, ugly, and had no reason to live. It was cyberbullying before we even had such a term, and I started to believe these people. In retrospect, I liken it to a sort of brainwashing. When you read about yourself on that laptop or on your cell phone, there seems to be a power in those words that's hard to explain. Maybe it's because you feel the whole world is reading all of it as well. And unless they protest what's being said, as far as you're concerned, they're in agreement. So the cruel comments grow credible in an eerie way, making you think what others are saying, mostly strangers, must be true. I believe that's why cyberbullying has such potential to be lethal, no matter what age. There was no escape from the torment. It seemed my life was ruined. Like so many who endure cyber-catastrophe today, I wanted to die. I had a plan on how to make that happen.

Luckily, faith, family and friends to the rescue, not just to help me survive, but to help me engage an inner strength I never knew I had to fight back. Three federal lawsuits later, I got control of my life back again. I was granted copyright ownership to all of those images from Key West, giving me legal means to at least stop the dissemination and get as much of that "mistake" off the Internet as possible. Truth is though, once it's out there, no matter how many times you hit delete, or take something down, to some degree, it's out there *forever and for all to see*. For me, that means my lawyers and other experts I hire can't get to those who run some sites on the dark side of the web, or obscure websites overseas violating my copyrights. I've come to terms with that.

## IAN ON IT:

This has always been a problem from the invention of copyright law. It's not that the copyright is difficult to secure. It's that the copyright is difficult to enforce. The largest companies with substantial resources have teams of ex-law enforcement whose sole job is to track down copyright infringers. They have several intellectual property firms on-call, ready to prosecute copyright pirates around the world. It is a costly part of business.

When a TV station in Cleveland, Ohio, a much bigger market than from where I was fired, recognized my resolve and gave me a second chance at my career, the healing could begin. I can't put into words what a blessing that was, and I'm eternally grateful to the station managers who believed in me.

With that, I worked my butt off, determined to prove to the world I was more than that one mistake. While I started there as a freelancer, it wasn't long before I would sign on full-time and make it back to the anchor desk. As cathartic as that was, it wasn't until various charities invited me back to take part in their events that I truly felt redeemed, sure the nightmare was over—the scandal was behind me. I consider any invite to work with charities such an honor. It would seem victory was mine over the monster that had come so close to claiming my life.

I learned quickly, however, victory can be short-lived if you're not wary. It's often something you need to continue to defend, just as athletes defend their titles. As resolved as I'd become to forgive myself and separate myself from my past, there were others just as determined to not let that happen. Emails would come in from viewers who wanted to make sure I knew that they knew my past and weren't about to forget or look beyond it. Sometimes the messages would come in letters in my real mailbox like this:

> KATHERINE "BimBo"
> So You Do SomEThinG STuPiD AND WANT
> To "SuE" WELL I HoPE You LoSE, WHAT A
> DumB THinG To Do, WHAT A DumBELL, You
> YES You NEED To PAY. I HoPE You
> LosE YouR JoB Too YoU AND THAT STuPiD
> ~~_____~~ You BoTH SHouLD BE FiRED
> GoNE DoNE FiNiTE oVER AND uNABLE To
> GET A JoB iN BroADcAsTing WHAT WERE You
> Two THinkiNG?

It would be when words like this no longer made me want to give up, but motivated me to do even better that I realized how much my ordeal had become part of me. It sunk in how much I had learned and grown from it. Most importantly, it occurred to me how much I don't want something like what happened with me, to happen to you.

You might be thinking, *She's talking about letting loose in some crazy escapade in Key West. Something like that IS NOT GOING TO HAPPEN TO ME.* I sure hope not, but what about these scenarios: What does it look like when you have a meltdown on your kids in the grocery store? When you lose your temper with a store clerk? Then there's the person we can all become when road rage gets the best of us. It can be something as simple as fighting with a flight attendant. What happens when those moments are captured in images that are shared on social media by a stranger, a text by a so-called friend who got a kick out of your weak moment, or an email by a co-worker?

It happens every day. Someone is shamed, mocked, or blatantly bullied online. A sort of scandal evolves when those who are compelled to follow along or join in magnify the mistake or the poor judgement. Sometimes it's exploitation of a mistake you made. It's the result of something you did to yourself like in my situation. All it takes is one misinterpreted email or text, a tweet gone bad, an irresponsible post or picture—one poor choicc, online or off, to undermine all you've worked for, wipe out your dreams, and drastically change life as you know it.

Or sometimes, you just happen to be the random target of cruelty. It could be through malicious words, GIFs, unflattering photos, or something as bad as a photo of your face added to an image of someone else's nude body, then shared like crazy. No one is immune, not you or those you care about. Not even your thriving business. Businesses are often unfairly battered online to the point of near impossible recovery.

It's a point you'll read about a lot in this book. Vulnerability to online or social media scandal is universal, whether you're a very private person or high-profile, a small business or a multi-million-dollar organization.

## IAN ON IT:

The important thing is to know when to draw the line—the line between the risks of being a public person and outright defamation. Defamation is a legal rule that allows someone whose reputation has been muddied, to sue the writer, speaker, or communicator for making the false statement. The key to such a suit is damages—the person who was defamed must have suffered cognizable and provable harm. Additionally, if you are a public figure, you have an even more difficult evidentiary burden. If you need to draw the line, you must be prepared for the large expense of hiring lawyers and long-time commitment of getting a case to trial. Justice moves slowly these days.

The correlation between the growing trend of online cruelty and the suicide rate in the U.S., at all ages, is clear. Things need to change. There are advocates, lawmakers, and other experts committed to that change. But until then, it's up to us, up to you, to stand steadfast in protecting yourselves and each other. We all need to be more vigilant on this relatively new front. But…what does that mean?

Think about how we use vigilance when it comes to something like protecting ourselves from crime, like always being aware of your surroundings. It's not much different when we're talking about protecting ourselves from cyber-catastrophe, really. As well, *should* you fall victim, the vigilance is similar to self-care while healing from any sort of injury or illness, it's about following the doctor's orders. I hope you find the advice and insight in the following chapters game-changing in how you incorporate vigilance while navigating our ever-evolving digital reality, especially social media.

I write this book in tribute to those who succumb to this new brand of humiliation that too often can seem insurmountable, and as an advocate for those who struggle with it every day—who are left wondering if there will be a tomorrow, like I did. This is one of those areas where one victim is one too many, and I truly believe, just as we're so quickly trained to master the next app, device, or other piece of technology, we can also master the practice of re-focusing past that screen to a different kind of reset—an updated mindfulness. I'm humbled and heartened to serve as living proof digital cruelty is survivable, one thoughtful choice at a time.

# CHAPTER 1:

# MY STORY, ABBREVIATED

## *It Starts with a Dream*

Maybe we took privacy for granted more before the Internet and the "dot com" explosion. We definitely knew to respect other's privacy, but it was not something we had to put so much thought into not long ago. We didn't have social media, or much of anything digital for that matter, to *make* us ponder privacy, or to monopolize so much of our daily lives. We had to find other ways to keep busy and to keep our minds occupied when we weren't hanging out with friends. Instead of being so preoccupied with devices and what others were doing, there was more room and more motivation to get to know ourselves better—like what we were good at, what we weren't so good at, and what we were passionate about. It entailed spending that downtime daydreaming about what our tomorrow might look like, instead of hours of mindless scroll sessions through empty calorie social media news feeds.

As a kid, growing up in Northeast Ohio, I was fascinated by TV news. When the other kids in the neighborhood were playing outside, I was in front of the TV watching the news.

*How do those people do it*, I wondered. *How do they find out all this information? How do they sit in front of a camera and talk with such ease, like they're talking to their friends? How does it feel to be on TV? To have the responsibility to inform everyone?*

I'll never forget that day I was watching the news with my grandmother, Nonny. I asked, "Nonny, do you think I could do the news someday?"

"Yes, honey," she said without hesitation, "I think you'd be wonderful at it."

Her response that day set my future into motion. The daydreaming soared to a whole new level. If Nonny, whose advice and opinions I cherished, believed in me, I was going to believe in me. TV news evolved into an intrigue I could not shake—my dream. Through high school and college, I kept my nose to the proverbial grindstone, and never—okay, rarely—strayed or did anything I shouldn't. I spent most of my free time learning all I could about broadcasting—every facet of it. The history, the changing technology, the business side of it, the production side of it, the role it plays in our society, the pros and cons of a life in TV news, and of course, most importantly, the journalism. I was obsessed.

During breaks in college, I'd go looking for any TV or

radio station that would let me hang out, maybe even do some work. I was willing to mop the floors if that's what it took to get in behind the scenes. That dedication paid off, especially going into my senior year in college when I landed an internship at a small TV station in Erie, Pennsylvania, less than an hour from my home. I was only supposed to be there for a few days a week. No pay. In fact, my parents paid my college for the internship credits. I was there almost every day that summer while still trying to hold down a part-time job as a department store cashier for gas and food money.

I don't think the station management understood what they were in for. I became an over-enthusiastic, overambitious pain in the butt intern, tagging along with any reporter I could for the day, watching over everyone's shoulders. I'd hang out with the assignment editor when I wasn't with a reporter, sometimes camp out in the control room, follow videographers, anchors, and producers, hounding them with questions, offering to complete any task at hand. I wanted to know details. I wanted to roll up my sleeves. Still, when the internship was over, they welcomed me back whenever I wanted. So, just about every time I came home from college, I'd make a beeline to good old WICU. I appealed for a job at the station so often that, finally, only a couple of months after I graduated from college, they gave in.

I did it! I was a reporter.

That's when the true test came. I was told by many it would be tough starting out. An understatement. Beginning in TV news, you typically move from city to city chasing after better positions, leaving behind family and friends. You work crazy hours, overnights, weekends, holidays. You work out in the snow, the sleet, the rain, the blistering heat. Someone's gotta do it, right? I can't tell you how many times I had to hide behind police car doors, covering stand-offs with the bad guys, knowing bullets could start flying anytime. Speaking of bad guys, one time, after covering a murder hearing in a small rural Pennsylvania town, a relative of the alleged killer chased me down in the parking lot. Taking her rage out on me for some reason, she shoved me and just before she was about to throw a fist, another relative stopped her. I was only a few months into the job. The danger, even at the small market level, is real.

And the money. Let me tell you—when you start in the business, the money is a joke. Every TV journalist has similar stories to share. But the more I learned and experienced the harsh realities of life in TV, the more dedicated and determined I grew, and the more in love with this dream I became. This was not a fling; this was a true commitment. For better or for worse. The reward of creating a journalistic piece that truly captured the spirit of the story, that informed, educated, and sometimes entertained, quickly became an addiction that, for me, far outweighed the challenges. There were plenty of tears and days of defeat too. But I knew inside I was dealing with growing pains (I can write an entire book on that!). Quitting was never an option.

Finally, about five years and three cities into my career, I landed a job back in my home state of Ohio, in little Youngstown. I was close to my hometown near Cleveland, and surrounded by family and friends once again, working a somewhat normal schedule, eventually becoming a full-time anchor, and making a respectable salary.

***

### *And a Screeching Halt…*

That also happens to be when my career had to take a back seat to my health. I was thirty-two when I had that doctor's visit that I remember all too well. I made the appointment because of a typical cold. As soon as he listened to my heart, the expression on his face made it clear there was something else going on.

"Doctor, everything okay?" I asked. "Just a cold, right?"

He pulled off the stethoscope, looking at me for a brief second as if searching for how to say something the right way. "Catherine, you might have a cold, yes, but I'm afraid we have a much bigger problem than that."

"What kind of problem?"

"It's a very distinct murmur," he went on. "You need to get further testing. I'm going to send you to the hospital for that."

As it turned out, I'd had a severely defective heart my whole life. I was told I'd be lucky to make it to forty if I didn't have it corrected. The only fix—open-heart surgery.

That kind of experience changes you. As I learned, you can choose whether it changes you for the better or the bitter worse. I chose for the better. After the recovery, I felt better than I had my entire life. The chronic fatigue which kept me from so much over the years, like sports, dissipated. I traded in sleeping as a favorite pastime, for exercise. Finally, I could really work out, as in run marathons, when running three miles was a tremendous struggle before the surgery, as much as I kept trying. It also gave me a new appreciation for so many of the people and other blessings in my life, including the crazy dream career. Most importantly, it gave me an understanding of what that kind of vulnerability feels like and an empathy I never knew before for others who were ill.

Eventually I got back to work. And, who knew? When I least expected it, I met "the" one, Rick, while running in the local park one afternoon. He had already run a marathon and would eventually help me train for my precious first 26.2-mile journey. He even ended up running the race with my brother and me. My next finish line with Rick would be at the altar. Getting married in my mid-thirties, living my dream career near family in my home state—my heart was more than healed, it was fuller than it had ever been.

Not even a year after we were married, though, another major health issue arose. I developed a rare lung disease that made the heart surgery pale in comparison. The disease took me from running a marathon to struggling to complete a sentence without coughing as my lungs spasmed. I could barely make it through a newscast. It got to the point that our producer had to give my co-anchor the majority of the stories to read. The pain and diffi- culty progressed with each day, and doctor after doctor could not figure it out. Finally, a specialist ordered a biopsy, which was no small procedure. It was full-blown surgery that required major incisions through my back and side in order to cut out a sample from my lung.

"Can you at least tell me if I'm going to make it?" I asked my doctor, jokingly.

"We need to take it one step at a time, one day at a time, my dear," he replied slowly and deliberately.

Not the response I was expecting. His words left us dumb-founded. I was in danger. I was rapidly losing my ability to breathe. And whatever was wrong, a cure wasn't coming soon, if at all. As a stop-gap measure, I was put on heavy doses of predni-sone, to bring the swelling in my lungs down and make me more comfortable.

Finally, after nearly two weeks, results of the biopsy came in. A deadly bacterial infection was filling my lungs. That called for a monstrous experimental drug regimen, including thousands of dollars' worth of specialized antibiotics each month, in addition to continuing the steroids.

My face blew up like a balloon, into what is referred to as a "moon face." The steroids put me on edge, I could barely sleep. Hearing my lungs crackling when I laid down didn't help. I learned exactly where my liver was, as pain set in from the drug toxicity. But the spasms started easing at least. I was starting to speak full sentences without coughing my way through, enough to return to work. I was so pleased and optimistic until driving to work one morning that first week back when I started sweating and gasping for air again, and felt a sharp pain in my chest. I could not make it through the newscast that morning without having to excuse myself from the set again and again to try to catch my breath, hoping to walk it off. As soon as the show was over, I called my lung specialist. He told me to get to the hospital right away.

The results of a CT scan were immediate. My doctor took me back to a small office in the imaging area. "Catherine, I have bad news and good news. What do you want first?"

"Good news please."

"Okay. The drugs are working—look here." He pointed to the scan images. "The tops of your lungs are clearing."

"They are?" Considering how bad I had felt, I was confused. "You're saying for sure, I'm going to live?"

He turned to me with his big brown eyes sparkling. "Yes, my dear, you are going to live. You have what's called non-tuber-culous mycobacterial disease." He referred back to the images. "It's stubborn and will become resistant to antibiotics, which means you'll have to switch up medicine every few weeks until it's completely gone. You'll also have to stay on prednisone."

Then, came the bad news I'd forgotten about.

"Your right lung—the one we took the biopsy from—is collapsed, which is why you're in so much pain. Your lung is leaking air from the biopsy incision. And that air surrounding the lung is crushing it. It needs to be aspirated."

He went on to explain how he had to insert a large needle and syringe between my ribs, through my chest wall, into my chest cavity to pull that air out. Normally, hearing that kind of talk would make for bad news. But I'd just learned I was going to live.

"No problem, let's do it."

***

## *A Celebration Like No Other*

Rick and I planned a trip to Key West, Florida to celebrate our one-year anniversary which coincided with the good news I was getting better. Still on heavy medication when we arrived, I couldn't drink much, which was fine with me. One evening, as we were walking down the main strip, Duval Street, in the middle of spring break, I was overcome by a sort of emotional inebriation. There were so many people out, excitement in the air, everyone seemed happy and carefree. The warm breeze felt delightful.

*Life is really good,* I thought.

Turning to my husband, I said, "I've got this second chance at life, I'm going to live it to the fullest and do things I would never have done before."

It just so happened that we walked into a bar that was about to host a wet T-shirt contest. Yep, a wet T-shirt contest. A traditional spring break event. I'd never even seen one. Neither had my husband. (At least that's what he said.) The former goodie two-shoes me would've scoffed at anyone who would let themselves be part of such objectification.

"Okay, ladies, we're looking for contestants," a man called out from the stage.

While watching this man on the stage working the crowd, those words I uttered just moments before started to play back in my head, *I'm going to do things I would've never done before.* That mindset, combined with taking a medication known to induce compulsive behavior made for the perfect storm. "I'll do it!" I heard myself yell out.

Boy, did I do it. I got caught up in the moment, and despite feeling very uncomfortable toward the end, when other contestants took everything off, my competitive spirit got the best of me. Ugh.

Walking back to the hotel, I was in tears, so disappointed in myself for getting carried away like that. Rick felt bad too after laughing through the entire thing knowing how much I was stepping out of character. So, we made a pact to leave it in Key West, learn from it, and never do anything like that again.

Back then, we all had the not-so-smart cell phones. We were just starting to take pictures on our mobile devices, which were mostly flip phones, but few knew what to do with those pictures. The images just stayed on our phones for the most part. There was no mainstream, instant upload social media back then. No Facebook, Twitter, Instagram, certainly nothing like Tik-Tok. My Space was about it, and it was far from the pervasive social media we know today. You couldn't share a photo or video with a couple taps to your phone. And texting—oh, it was a whole different game back then. It was complicated. The average person wasn't able to send or receive texts with photos, let alone video. There was, however, the foundation of it all. The Internet.

Little did I know a few people from a couple of popular websites were there documenting the whole thing. One was a photographer who snapped dozens of pictures which could be easily shared from one website to another. As if that wasn't bad enough, there was that one site similar to *Girls Gone Wild* that took the bad dream to a full-blown nightmare. *Girls Gone Wild* was an infamous multi-million-dollar video production operation that was extremely well-known in the late 1990s and early 2000s. Staff sought out young women, especially college aged women, getting drunk and wild, often exposing themselves, even getting sexual, in public, as well as in more private situations. They filmed them and sold the videos with a remarkable late night TV marketing campaign. They've been accused of coaxing women into doing things they wouldn't have normally done and filming women who were underage. The owner of the now defunct company landed in a lot of trouble over the years—jail time.

The company that caught me in video in my unfortunate "gone wild," moment was a "want to be" *Girls Gone Wild*, working on a smaller level, producing videos of women cutting loose at various partying events. Like *Girls Gone Wild*, they packaged up those videos and sold them online, VHS or DVD, customer's choice.

\*\*\*

### *The Nightmare Begins*

That Christmas, nearly ten months later, was a special holiday for us as we reflected on the previous Christmas when the lung illness had been at its worst and we didn't know if I'd survive. By then, we'd mostly put that night in Key West behind us. While running around the house taking care of all the details in getting ready for our party, I noticed there was a message on our answering machine. When I hit play, the world came to a stand-still.

"Hi, Rick and Catherine—"

I had no idea who this woman was. Her tone turned vicious. "Just want to let you know the video from *Girls Gone Wild* has hit the Youngstown area. You're being shown, Catherine, or Cathy from Kent, I guess that's your stage name, everywhere from Channel 21 to Irish Bob's and Royal Oaks Bar and Grill."

My heart started racing.

"Everyone has seen you in your full entire. Honey, your days are over. You think you're such a prissy little bitch, but your days are over. Have a very Merry Christmas."

Click.

I knew immediately what she was talking about, especially when she called me, "Cathy from Kent." That's the name I playfully used that night when the participants were asked their names and where they went to college.

I felt paralyzed and panicked. Standing in the living room, I called out to Rick in the kitchen as calmly as I could, trying not to alarm my stepdaughters, who were eighteen and twenty at the time. When I handed him the phone to listen to the message, his face dropped. Somehow, we went on with the party, keeping our anguish mostly between us.

I had no choice but to tell my boss the next day. Soon after, I lost my job. My dream job, what I'd wanted since I was a kid, what I had worked tirelessly for. A career shattered. The downward spiral would begin. My story became national news as I was hounded by the media worldwide. The theme became "girl next door turns girl gone wild." I even became the topic of *David Letterman's Top Ten List: The 10 Best Things About Having a Stripper as an Anchor*. I was chased down in public by people blurting out vile comments like, "Hey Catherine, take it off. Show us your tits!" Even our home was no place to hide. Cars would slow down in front of our house with people honking their horns and yelling awful things out their windows.

It got to the point where my only true source of comfort was in that bottom drawer where we kept leftover prescription pain medication. Powerful stuff. That would do the job. Many nights I'd lay in bed with my mind on that drawer thinking, *tomorrow will be the day, tomorrow I'll use the drawer*.

Thank God, *that* tomorrow never happened, instead with each day comes more realization of just how blessed I am. That's especially true when I think of the incredible faith, family, and friends embracing and protecting me through it all. Seventeen years later, I can look back on what I called a nightmare recognizing how much it *gave* me. It made for a stronger, wiser, more empathetic me. Most importantly, it gives me precious, unique insight to share with the world.

*** 

### *Making It Count!*

As a journalist, you have a sense of responsibility to make a difference. One of the best ways to do that is through storytelling, in hopes that others are, at best, inspired by, and at least, informed and educated by the stories you have the privilege of sharing.

A couple of years after my own crazy story I managed to reclaim my dream career in a much bigger market from where I was let go, and even closer to my Cleveland area home. There are many to thank for helping make that happen. But sitting on the news set telling more stories about others—kids, in particular—taking their own lives as the result of cyber-cruelty left me with a gnawing ache inside, almost a feeling of guilt. I realized it stemmed from the idea that maybe, just maybe, if I would've had the chance to talk to these young people, I could've offered them just enough hope to get through. I know the hopelessness. I also know reason for hopefulness isn't far behind. It became clear to me I needed to take action. I needed to organize and share my unique insight on all this, put it out there in a way that would caution and guide, yet inspire. My desire and ability to make a difference has led me beyond journalism to speaking events, including a TEDx Talk, a couple of books, coaching, and consulting. A chance to truly help. A mission to make it count, as I believe every struggle in life counts for something, somehow.

So, with every episode of tumult endured comes prime and precious opportunity to spread those wings a bit further and realize a new dream.

# CHAPTER 2:

# MYTH: THERE'S PRIVACY ONLINE

"Don't worry—just my close circle of friends can see it. I have my security settings on private." It drives me crazy when I come across a risqué post or picture on someone's social media page, and when I bring it to their attention they chuckle and respond with something like the above. Don't they understand? There is *no* privacy online. Nightmare potential is real with some of the most seemingly innocuous posts.

Ashley can tell you all about it. The twenty-four-year-old from Georgia was with a friend on a European trip when someone took a picture of her living it up. A big beautiful smile, a bright red top to match her lipstick, her shiny strawberry blonde hair just hitting her shoulders. She's holding both hands up to the camera. One holding a glass of red wine, the other holding what appears to be a beer. She decided to post the picture on her "private"

Facebook page. She was a teacher. So, guess what happened. She lost her dream job.

Her lawyer, Richard Storrs, remembers the case well, including how deeply hurt she was after losing a job she was passionate about. More so, he recalls how shocked she was that this could have happened. He stresses she always maintained the highest-level privacy settings on her Facebook account, specifically to make sure neither students nor parents could gain access. Somehow, though, that particular picture circulated around enough to get back to her principal. Storrs represented her in her suit over losing her job. But that brought to the surface another post never meant to be seen by anyone other than her "friends." Storrs explains it was a post which included profanity. She mentioned a game known as "Crazy Bitch Bingo." She lost the lawsuit and made the national news. It was determined the picture "promoted alcohol use." That, combined with allowing her page to contain profanity, resulted in the ruling that she violated warnings about "unacceptable online activities." Scandal? You bet.

**IAN ON IT:**

Increasingly, businesses are adopting "social media policies" and including them to be reviewed and acknowledged in hiring documents. These rules should be adhered to. Courts have upheld the appropriateness of these policies as within the legitimate discretion of an employer.

**Additionally, if you work within an environment in which you interact with children, courts scrutinize employee conduct and uphold terminations based on violations of social media rules with expanding frequency.**

Did Ashley make a mistake that night on vacation by deciding to double fist her booze in the first place? Did she make a mistake by allowing the photograph to be taken? Who's to say? Who's to judge? Well, except for the judge who presided over her case, I guess. Her real mistake and poor judgement came in when she trusted that there was such a thing as privacy in the digi-sphere. To this day, even her lawyer is not sure who might have shared, or leaked, that picture. Maybe the privacy settings failed her, maybe a "frenemy" had access to her account. But the good news is, according to her attorney, it didn't take her too long to bounce back and get on with her life. She went on to graduate school, and was apparently able to reclaim and advance her career in education. But, certainly, lesson learned.

\*\*\*

Then there's the case of Michael. From the time he was little he loved performing and was very gifted at acting, singing, and dancing. His dream was to become a world-class performer. During his last year in college, one of his auditions went especially well, and he received the phone call he had been waiting for his entire life, from one of the top production companies in the country.

"Michael, we like what we see. You'll have a job with us when you graduate." You can imagine how thrilled he was.

Not long after, he was hanging out with his girlfriend, who had a unique hobby. She designed bongs out of various bottles. Pieces of art, some would say. One day, she took a picture of Michael holding one of her masterpieces, proudly displaying her work, even though he never took part in bong use and never intended to. She posted the photo on her "private" Facebook page, knowing their small circle of mutual friends would get a kick out of it because it is SO not him. One friend was so amused, he wanted to share with a couple other friends. Nope, he couldn't do that because of the girlfriend's Facebook page security settings. But that didn't stop him because there's always the *screenshot* to get around that. So, he took a screenshot of it, shared it with a few friends, who then shared it with strangers. Suddenly, this picture Michael and his girlfriend thought made for a fun private joke with just their close friends, was all over social media.

Michael didn't think much of it after the initial embarrassment. He went on to graduate, but as he was packing his bags to go claim that dream job, the phone rang.

"Michael?" the voice on the other end said—a very serious tone.

"Yes, this is Michael."

"Michael, I'm sorry we're going to have to rescind our offer. We came across some information that indicates you don't quite fit our brand. Good luck in your future endeavors."

Click.

Poof.

Michael's dream, gone, at least for the moment, because he thought there was privacy online. That picture, now, potentially attached to him *forever and for all to see.*

Screenshots can be so convenient. I use them often, for various purposes. But they're dangerous on a number of levels. If we ever had anything that resembled privacy in the digital world, especially on the social level, the screenshot alone wipes it out. Plus, since they're so easy to capture, the legal ramifications are often the last thing on our minds. While Michael suffered consequences of believing there is privacy online, those who had fun with the screenshot apparently dodged their own serious consequences—a lawsuit for copyright infringement. That picture belonged to Michael and/or his girlfriend. That means no one else had the right to use it as they did.

**IAN ON IT:**

One of the bundles of copyrights you receive when you create art is the right to duplicate your creations. If someone copies your creation without your permission, technically, they are infringing your copyright. A screenshot is a "copy" of an online work of art. Therefore, a court is justified in concluding that a screenshot can be an unlawful infringement.

There's also this to consider. The cloud. The cloud idea gives us that sense of security that our valuable information is stored away safely, to be retrieved only by you when you want it. While I'm far from being an expert when it comes to technology, here's a red flag that's easy to spot if you think about this kind of stuff as much as I do. For most of us, as soon as we take a photo on our cell phones, it goes right up to the cloud, whatever cloud that might be for you. That means that image is essentially shared automatically, without us having to hit share, or send, or enter, or anything. Again, convenient, right? Hold on. All you have to do is a Google search on clouds being hacked to see they are *not* foolproof.

Remember when the iCloud was hacked in 2014? Talk about scandal. Big celebs like Jennifer Lawrence, Kate Upton, and Rihanna were violated. What were intended to be private images became available to the world. Sure, celebs are different to an extent. There is a so-called "market," or audience that really wants to see these behind the scenes, or vulnerable moments of entertainers. Big demand equals big viral potential. That would be on a national, if not global, level. When it comes to the rest of us, though, something about you doesn't need to go viral globally for it to make your life a humiliation hell. It just needs to go viral amongst your friends, co-workers, classmates, and community, in your own circle of the world for it to wreak havoc.

So you might want to ask yourself, with every single picture you take, *How would I feel if the rest of my world saw it?* I'm talking people like your grandmother, your pastor, your boss, your teacher. Most likely, most of your pictures are benign and harmless. But there are those times when photos are taken during silly, irresponsible moments. We like to think those pictures will stay private but, the reality is, as soon as they're taken, those moments are no longer guaranteed to stay private. They are shared in the cloud. Who knows how else they might make the rounds someday, somehow?

**IAN ON IT:**

**Using the services of a lawyer, you technically could get an injunction against the publication of your online creation. However, in real life, the spread of online creation shares is so fast and pervasive, getting your art back in your private portfolio is like attempting to put toothpaste back in the tube.**

During my fiasco, I can't tell you how many people said to me, "I'm so glad we didn't have cell phone cameras back when I was young. If there were pictures of my crazy times, I would be in big trouble."

Sometimes it's best not to capture moments digitally, but just to experience them, be present in them, and enjoy them without the distraction of having to take out that cell phone for pictures. That's especially true when they're moments you know you wouldn't want to share with the world. They may be fun times with people who you trust explicitly, but not your proudest times. Those times happen in all our lives: celebrating, sulking, too much letting loose, times when we step out of character. How about letting your memory do the picture taking? Maybe such a moment didn't seem as bad in your recollection, but pictures during those times reveal a harsh dose of reality you really don't need, and certainly don't need to have documented for others to potentially see—to potentially stir up scandal, sometimes years later. Also, there are times when those flashbacks actually look better in your memory than they would in an electronic image, anyway. Think about how you remember your childhood home without photos. It's probably a lot bigger in your memory than it really was. What's wrong with letting it stay the way you remember and cherish it?

Then there's the dreaded lost, stolen, or hacked cell phone. It happens all the time, and no one thinks it's going to happen to them. We all know the sick and freaked out feeling when it does happen. You get home after a long, full day of running around, maybe errands, maybe work, you finally get to sit down and catch your breath. You reach for your phone and it's not there! You dig through every pocket, empty out your purse, and start to feel hot and shaky. *This isn't happening!* You run to the car, search under the seats, prod through every nook and cranny in your car. Nothing. Now, you need your phone to tell someone that it's missing, you need to start calling the places where you were earlier. Oh boy. I'm feeling my heart beat faster and my stomach knotting just writing this scenario. Panic.

Our mobile devices have become an extension of us, and

in a big way, so that feeling we experience when this happens is raw vulnerability, isn't it? Suddenly you feel jarringly lost without your precious device that you know so well. Then, the dread of having to replace it sets in. And—it gets personal. Thoughts of violation kick in especially when you research how easy some tech geeks say it is to bypass lock screens, if you even use one. We start to take inventory of all the information stored on that phone and imagine someone else scrolling through it, clicking around, soaking it all in, maybe sharing with others. Shoot, our phones are basically our contemporary diaries, meant for our eyes only. You might think about those pictures on your phone, first. Those pictures you took during a wild time with friends, or a personal moment, maybe intimate pictures NEVER meant to go beyond your phone (even though they did go to the cloud the moment you took them).

Then, how about the email and text messages that can be found on your phone—the ones meant to remain solely between you and the person you were corresponding with? Messages can say a lot about who you are, what you're thinking, good and bad, sometimes about friends, family members, or your workplace. The list is endless. Then, finally, we think about the data that person can get to that jeopardizes your security, things like passwords, credit card information, banking accounts, and medical information.

A woman I know, Katelyn, recalls how she took nude photos of herself to text—or *sext*—to her then boyfriend. Sometime later, after she and her boyfriend broke up, she received a call from a friend who had come across those pictures online. On a porn-like site. In fact, those pictures were suddenly going viral in Katelyn's world. Turns out, she says, her ex-boyfriend's phone was stolen, and the thief easily found the images, and went to town sharing them.

Imagine the humiliation she endured. Unfortunately, I know it well. You feel like everyone in the world has seen you like that. You go to the grocery store and you feel everyone looking at you, recognizing you from the most compromising photos. You go out to dinner, you pump gas, you go for a walk in the park, there's no escaping that feeling of paranoia you never thought could be you. It's scandal in its very beginning stages.

Just about anything that can happen with a cell phone can happen with a laptop as well. They are, of course, not as much an additional appendage for most of us as our phones, and maybe don't have quite as much of a diary nature to them. But they do hold a great deal of data that you would like to think private, and no one else's business. If you tote around your laptop, losing it or having it stolen puts into motion all the anguish that goes with a missing cell phone. Suddenly, all that was meant to be private on that machine is essentially up for grabs—at risk of being shared with the world. Some laptops never leave the house. That doesn't make them insusceptible to violation. We all know, of course, there are extremely talented hackers who can find their way into even the most secure systems. But there's something else to consider with the stay at home laptop as well. Are you taking the precautions you need to keep it physically secured? I'm not just talking about keeping it locked away from a burglar. Unfortunately, you need to think about other people who come and go who might find it tempting, or convenient to jump on your computer to look something up, and happen upon other information you never expected anyone else to see.

The former mayor of a small town in British Columbia can tell you all about that. During my crisis, I was suddenly super aware of other people's digital disaster stories, cases making it clearer every day how little privacy we have with the invasive nature of our new and improved technology. Hers is one I remember well, because she made what is arguably a poor judgement call like mine that turned into a similar scandal. Excited to be the first female mayor in the small mill town, she had her husband take pictures of her in her new top office. In those photos, she wore the mayor's medal around her neck, a chain of office that's supposed to be worn during official mayoral events. She also wore a big smile. And that's *all* she wore. Yep, she took nude photos in the mayor's chambers that were meant, of course, only for herself and her husband to see, she explained in several reports. She apparently had confidence those pictures would remain private, on her home computer. Their intimate secret. Suddenly, they're on everyone else's computers too, via the Internet. How did that happen? Get this, it's believed some of her kid's friends found them on her computer during a house party. They stole them, and passed them around.

In various interviews she remained steadfast that she did not mean any "disgrace to the office." Despite pressure to resign, she stayed on, insisting she was the victim and went on to become reelected. One website, SFGATE.com, quotes her as saying, "It was a private moment and that's all it was." No matter what anyone might think about her because of that moment she had, it seems, most of all she was appalled that her privacy was violated. You can certainly understand that. Of course, that kind of shock was much more unexpected back in 2003 and 2004, when her scandal broke.

It's sad, but with each passing day it becomes clearer that there is no privacy in our digital world no matter how we adjust our privacy settings, no matter how secure our passwords might be. If you document a moment digital style, whether it's with a photo, a text message, an email, a direct message on social media, a snapchat, a TikTok, whatever, the biggest mistake you can make is assuming it's guaranteed to stay private. On the contrary, it is fair game, immediately. If you want to be guaranteed such moments stay private, don't snap the picture (at least not on your easily misplaced cellphone), don't send the text, comment, email, or DM. Resorting to good old-fashioned, person-to-person communication—face-to-face or even a phone conversation—to express yourself is the best option we have to keep private, private, as it should be.

**IAN ON IT:**

You can reduce the spread of online creations with lawyers, but you can't completely erase an image from the Internet, unless you are maybe Bill Gates?

With every stroke of the keyboard, on your laptop or on your cell phone, you are taking a chance. To keep the risk minimized, it's so good to be aware of what *can* happen when we lean too much toward believing the myth that there is privacy in our world of digital everything.

# CHAPTER 3:

# PICTURES AND POSTS

# WE CAN CONTROL

When you realize your dream, whether it's something that's come to you as the result of life's experiences, or something that's been inside you for as long as you can remember, you need to protect it with everything you have. One thing no one has though—total control. Staying focused, making the right choices, always keeping an eye out for opportunity and never giving up are great ways to feel like you're in the driver's seat. However, as much as we try our best to be our best and shoot for the stars, often, as the saying goes—*Life happens.* Unexpected hiccups in life remind us how little control we actually possess, and how easily any big plan can be thwarted. Often, though, the setbacks are temporary, or perhaps, even for the better. (Life is funny that way, isn't it?)

My husband's favorite line is, "It's going to be okay." Then he goes on with the rhetorical, "Why?" only to answer himself with the statement that says it all. "Because it has to be." While that is certainly meant to bring comfort during a trying situation, which it often does for me, (also, of course, knowing the Big Guy upstairs is really the one behind the wheel) it also drives home the point, with those few things we *can* control, we have a responsibility to step it up. Take control with the pictures and posts you *allow* yourself to be part of. Simply being vigilant can spare so much unnecessary grief.

## SELFIE-MANIA

Never before have we had such power to sabotage ourselves in a virtual split-second than we do right now. And, we do exactly that. One of the most popular tools we use to do that is the almighty selfie. Selfie-mania is part of our world, and it seems it's not going away anytime soon. Some people depend on the selfie, cannot go a day without taking one or two, or twenty, to let the world know exactly how they're doing, what they're doing and who they're doing it with. Why? The selfie prone will say, "Why not?" Fair response. Everyone has their thing, right? For some people life is all about the chance to capture a selfie. It's as if their experiences aren't really happening if there's not a selfie to share as proof. It's been referred to as "selfie-itis." People die, literally, in their attempts to get the perfect selfie. That's a whole separate book, but worth a Google search. Let's *face* it though, there are some pros to the selfie phenomenon. Some experts say it's a way to build confidence. Maybe a way to connect on a unique level. (Others say it can destroy confidence. Ugh, who knows?). They might have potential to boost your image, and take you to the next level in your social media status. The craze has, indeed, launched some people to social media fame. The right selfie work might open up other opportunities that otherwise might not have happened.

Capturing the perfect selfie can be an advanced artform in some respects. Okay, maybe that's pushing it a bit. However, the selfie pros work to find the right angle, the right makeup, the right location, the right lighting, and you can't leave out the importance of the right filter. Or, the perfect selfie, if there is such a thing, can be something as simple as capturing the right emotion. Typically, the success of a selfie is measured by how swiftly it permeates the digi-sphere, or trends on social media—the forwards, likes, shares, the retweets.

I take part too. Oh yeah, I see the fun in it, how much fun is a group selfie? I call it a "selfie party." And I enjoy having a few selfie parties with audience members at my speaking events. Something about it makes us all laugh, and seeing others laugh tops my list of favorites in life. When you think about it, though, the more others communicate with the world via selfie, the more pressure there is to keep the conversation going by selfie'ing back. Maybe it's a way to stay in the so-called game—keeps you relevant to some degree.

You have to admire the best selfie'ers when it comes to a

certain skill set as well as the determination to get that *best selfie ever*—no matter the cost. At the same time, I admire those who just say "no," and put more value in living in the present. Also, it seems selfie addiction is a thing. Something to be mindful of.

Despite any opinion on selfies, the fact is the wrong selfie, or genre of selfies, can also do serious damage. For the most part, selfies are what you are willing to show the world about yourself, when you show the wrong thing—again, *your choice*—that image becomes even more potent. It's not about what *others* are saying about you, whereas you might be able to argue something is taken out of context, or you were exploited or betrayed. A selfie represents what *you* are saying about you to the world that's going to be out there *forever and for all to see*. A simple, maybe corny, way to prevent selfie style self-sabotage is to keep this phrase in the back of your mind, HAPPY, HEALTHY SELFIE.

## THE HAPPY, HEALTHY SELFIE

### *Why Happy?*

Why put up a selfie that radiates anything other than "feel good?" Isn't there enough bad, sad and mad in the world? No need to contribute to negativity. It can be tempting to selfie your down moments and post away as a knee-jerk reaction seeking a little support or compassion, some sort of immediate fix from someone, anyone out there who happens to be listening via social media. The next day though, when whatever was bothering you is not as bad as you thought, because we all know it's often not, you look back at that selfie and a few things can happen. That negative feeling you documented in your unhappy selfie can certainly bring you back to that place you worked your way out of. Or, you could feel like a fool for putting yourself out there when you didn't even give yourself time to sort things out. And now that picture is *forever and for all to see*, especially if it was shared or retweeted. Or, worse, instead of comments from people on your side, meaning to help you, cruel comments populate that post, which brings on a whole new hurt. So often, when we put negativity out there, it finds its way back to our lives. That's not a chance worth taking. Social media is never a safe place to work out or air out real issues. That's what real people are for.

## *The Healthy Checklist*

You can keep those selfies healthy by taking inventory of everything going on in them. Like I said earlier, there are so few things in life we have control over. Fortunately, you are the boss with selfies—they're an extension of you, inherent in the word *selfie* itself. It's something to take advantage of at any age, or wherever you are in life. Let's talk about taking control with the three levels of inventory with pictures.

1. What's going on in the setting, or your surroundings? Is there a sleazy bar behind you? Are there a bunch of empty beer or wine bottles? What kind of signage is behind you? You can be linked to whatever is in the background of your picture, even if it's subliminally.

So, look closely at what's going on in the background that you don't want to be associated with.

2.    What are other people doing in this picture? Are there distasteful hand gestures, or hand gestures some people, like future employers, might not be familiar with? That could turn them off real fast. (I don't allow *any* hand gestures in my selfies, not taking any chances.) Are others making crazy faces that might be interpreted as drunk, or simply questionable characters you're hanging out with? Anything like that can manifest as a bad reflection on you. You've heard the saying "guilty by association," right?

3.    What are you doing in the picture that might be misinterpreted, or say something about you that you don't want to be part of your *forever and for all to see*? As an example, think of the story of Michael from Chapter 2. Remember how he and his girlfriend posted a photo of him with a bong, presumably smoking weed? It may have been a joke, because he would never really do that. But to those who don't know him the selfie says otherwise, which is how it cost him his big break in show business.

# PICTURES ARE WORTH A THOUSAND WORDS, AND THEN SOME...

You've heard the saying "pictures are worth a thousand words." That phrase can provide precious guidance in how to know which pictures are safe to post, and which you should keep to yourself as much as possible. Let's consider a few examples:

## *Mixed Messages: The Story of One Instagram Account*

What would you make of this? A young woman graduates from college and posts a beautiful picture of herself with a black cap and gown, and an honor cord draped around her neck, holding up her degree. She's got a big beautiful smile, with her glistening dark hair falling on her shoulders. Just behind her, the big stage she just walked across. What words come to mind? Maybe **successful, educated, smart, a go-getter.** Good stuff.

Another photo on her account is an action shot. She is captured in perfect form, mid-jump, spiking the ball over the net while playing on her college volleyball team. What words? How about **athletic, team player, committed?** Again, good stuff.

Then there's the picture from her high school graduation, with her red cap and gown. The gown is open enough to see her sweet, off-white lacy dress, and she's standing between her grandparents, arms around one another. Looks like it's in a modest living room. Big smiles. The words? I think of words like **love, family, wholesome**. Yep, more good stuff.

This makes for an attractive image in many ways. It could

certainly benefit her when she's applying to get into graduate school or trying to get a scholarship to continue her education, or maybe she's up for an award which considers her character. This is all thumbs up material for a potential employer as well. Pretty important when you'd assume she put all that hard work in at college to set herself up to claim that dream career.

Then, you click through the account a little further and, uh oh. There's a picture of her scantily clad in tiny red velvet shorts and a matching corset. She's sitting on the corner of a countertop, one leg over each side, her back arched and behind protruding, looking over her shoulder to the camera with a pouty face. What are some of the words you start to think of now?

Click again, and there she is in a skintight camouflage skirt, so short it barely covers her butt, which she has positioned toward the camera as the highlight of the photo. Her high heeled, open toe shoes have laces that wrap up to her knees. A flimsy black top drapes off her shoulders, baring most of her back. With her chest turned away, she's gazing over one shoulder to the camera, holding out the end of her long ponytail, with lips in full pout. Your words now? She has several more pictures like this throughout the account.

Sexy can be fun. Of all people, I get it. I did sexy on steroids, remember? Also, she's a beautiful young lady with a great figure. Pictures like the latter, though, are creating an image that will arguably work against her if she's serious about kicking off a respectable career, or any of those other scenarios I mentioned earlier: getting into grad school, up for a scholarship, etc. They will void out the smart, athletic, family person image we get from the previous photos. Show most any employer this account, and it might not seem fair, but unless they're looking for a lingerie model or someone with over-the-top sex appeal, they're probably going to pass on her.

A survey done by CareerBuilder.com recently revealed an estimated 70% of employers snoop on candidates' social media sites as part of the screening process. More than 50% report passing on a candidate for what they found there. As for what exactly made them pass, topping the list is provocative or inappropriate photos or videos. Next—pictures or information suggesting alcohol or drug use.

### *Alcohol and Social Media Don't Mix*

Speaking of that, on a middle-aged man's Facebook page there's a picture of him in a bar, holding up a huge mug of beer, maybe a twenty-six ouncer. What are some of the words or thoughts that come to mind when you come across it? Simple. Things like this guy **likes beer**, **bottoms up, R & R**. Now, add to that picture this caption "First one's almost gone, can't wait for the next." What are some of your thoughts as you glance at the photo again? If that frothy full mug he's holding is almost gone, doesn't it intimate that he's going to **guzzle**? And then there'll be a number two, just like number one and maybe he's on a **binge**. The person in this photo is someone I know. A good, kind, hard-working, responsible man, who was on his first day of a well-deserved vacation. He's doing what so many adults do on vacation. They belly-up to enjoy the first celebration beverage. Sometimes that's the best tasting drink of the year. Nothing wrong with that. Just taking a picture to hold onto the memory, sure, understandable. But posting it for the world to see with such a caption is opening him up for challenges no one needs. What if he's a candidate for a new job and the human resources manager comes across that picture while vetting him, and there are other candidates just as qualified for the position who don't have social media pictures involving booze? Who's going to get the job? Or, what if he's on the dating scene and someone who might be perfect for him sees that front and center when she does an internet search on him, like Googling his name? Can you see the red flags that might arise? It's so easy to convey the wrong impression in one photo which is why going through the healthy photo checklist above is always a good idea. That includes an objective look at your selfie, or any other picture you allow yourself to be part of and thinking about what words might come to people's minds if they have no idea of the context in which it was taken.

Many people's social media pages ooze booze. It's easy to see why. "Cheers" bring on cheer, right? It's called happy hour for a reason. What's wrong with showing the world your good times? By now, you know I'm all for putting good stuff out there. Then, you have the fact that booze is served up in so many picture-perfect ways. You have the beautifully packaged wine and beer bottles, then, oh, those fancy wine glasses. I love a quality wine glass, especially an oversized red wine glass. You've got the champagne flutes, classic martini glasses, curvy daiquiri glasses, good old-fashioned bourbon tumblers. Goblets galore! Even the right flask has a certain character, enough to be a collector's item.

You have the coolest looking beer mugs, topped off by the perfect froth. Who wouldn't want a photo with these stars?

Wait, though. Enjoying the aesthetics, and the rest of what comes with our adult beverages is one thing. Documenting your indulgence for your friends or followers, and everyone else, via photos, or even boasting about your boozeful bliss in words alone, is a whole different thing. What good does it do, really? In fact, it can result in a lot more than a bad hangover. I mentioned with my friend's photo how it can get in the way of a professional or romantic opportunity. That can be damaging enough, but there's so much more.

I know people who post picture after picture on their social media featuring their wine, beer, or liquor du jour. You might know of some people who do that too. I'm talking people who are responsible drinkers, who don't have a drinking problem at all. All it takes is a few spirited photos to give the wrong impression—and then some.

What happens when these people find themselves in trouble for something, maybe accused of something they're innocent of, they get sued for something, they find themselves in a bitter divorce or custody battle, or they do get busted for drunk driving, God forbid, hurt someone else? There's big risk the other side will find every picture with booze and use it against them to raise questions about their character. No joke. Suddenly a happy hour translates into your worst hour.

No matter what, evidence of anyone drinking a lot or often, or both, doesn't bode well. Recently, the Federal Rules of Evidence were amended to make social media content admissible in legal cases, and it doesn't even require an expert to authenticate most material. The last thing you want to do is explain why there are so many pictures on your social media featuring you with cocktails. Then there's the possibility *you* launch a case against someone else that ends up in court. How are you going to look when the defendant finds a reason to include in their exhibits all the photos you posted with alcohol? It's not going to fare in your favor, but also, imagine how that's going to feel when they're put up on a big screen for the judge and jury to scrutinize, whether you're the defendant *or* the plaintiff. I know how something like that can feel. Think of the pictures of me that were put before judge and jury. I wouldn't wish that kind of humiliation upon anyone. Your drinks don't have to be heavy-duty for the pictures of you with them to knock you on your ass.

Also worth noting on this topic, when you are drinking, taking part in marijuana use or using anything that messes with your head, including pain meds, stay away from your cell phone or computer. We all know emotions can kick in during those times. That means doing or saying things that could be super regretful is a real possibility. It gets so much worse if you expose your inebriation digitally, basically putting it on record. How about turning your phone over to someone else when the drinks start flowing, just like you might hand your keys over? My husband and I check each other on that. When one of us takes our cell phone out while enjoying a cocktail, the other always makes sure it's just to scroll, never to send.

## *Peer Pressure Peril in Pictures*

It's a salute to remember, for all the wrong reasons. At first glance, it looks like a fun high school memory in the making. A photo of a bunch of high school boys, dressed up in front of a courthouse. All smiles. Then, you realize what's going on here—it's shocking. They're all giving the same gesture. Of all things, they're giving the Nazi salute. Sadly, it's the picture that put little Baraboo, Wisconsin on the map in 2018. Absolute scandal.

The story is these young men were on their way to the junior prom. A dad offered to take a photo of them all spiffed up and excited for the fun to begin. Most of us can relate to that because it's one of those moments that bonds lifelong classmates, especially in small-town U.S.A. Apparently, just before taking the photo, the dad said something that influenced them to give the Nazi salute, or "throw it up," as it was described in one Tweet with the photo, accompanied by #Barabooproud. That dad posted the photo on his social media and it went viral. It made news around the country. While he reportedly apologized calling it just a "joke," he also deleted it from his pages.

When I was hired to speak in a town near Baraboo, someone brought this story to my attention. Despite the originals being deleted from the dad's account, it took me only a few seconds to find that heartbreaking photo. There's no taking something like that back. If you zoom in on the photo, each of the guys is absolutely recognizable. That means this picture is part of their *forever and for all to see*. Maybe at the time they didn't quite understand what that gesture stands for. That's what I'd like to think. But they sure do know now, and are reportedly still having to answer for it. It's often used as an example of how racism and anti-Semitism still run strong in the U.S. Nonetheless, this is a picture each of them ALLOWED himself to be a part of. They had the option of saying, "No."

Up in the right-hand corner, one young man stands out. He's one of only a few who did not take part. He's not even smiling. He reportedly said he didn't want any part of it, but it happened so fast, he didn't have time to get out of the shot. Good for him, but it's unfortunate he has to be associated with it at all.

Have you ever had something like this happen? You're in a situation you might not be comfortable with and suddenly others start taking pictures. Off the top of my mind, I'm thinking about a party or joke that gets out of hand, a group of high school students skipping class, or taking part in something that could get them in hot water. It seemed fun at first, but then turned reckless, or mean-spirited. Think of hazing situations like making someone drink too much or daring someone to do something crazy dangerous, and they do it purely out of pressure. When the so-called "herd mentality" takes over, situations can escalate quickly into something you never expected and would never want to be associated with. This is when you need to take control. Sound off that you don't want to be photographed and do your best to turn your face away from any camera pointed in your direction, or find a way to obscure it and get out of the situation right away. There's a good chance your protest will make others second guess their participation as well, not to mention documentation of it. You might not be the most popular person for standing your ground, but when it's for the sake of your *forever and for all to see*, trust me, it will be worth it.

## Safe Sexting: No Such Thing

*Your Guide to Safer Sexting, Here's How to Sext Safely, Tips on How to Practice Safe Sexting.* Yep, you can find article after article suggesting there are ways to engage in safe sexting.

Safe sexting? Really? I shake my head. I mean, I *really* shake my head. Some might suggest sending nudes that don't show your face, and you'll never get caught. Brilliant! Except for the fact most every picture taken on a cell phone has an embedded code that can potentially track it right back to you, or at least to whomever owns the phone it was taken on. A quick online search will tell you all about that, as well as how to remove the code.

Again, brilliant! Just remove the code and you're good to go, right? Nope. No way. Not at all.

Don't get me wrong, I'm certainly not judging those who want to get in on the action. I get the fascination. The glaring problem with it, though, is the risk, serious risk. Say you take every precaution on the technical end—which can be quite involved—there are simply too many things that can go wrong on the human end. And do they ever.

There are countless cases of sexting gone wrong. The life-changing type of gone wrong. The case of Lauren comes to mind first. A twenty-five-year-old outstanding middle school math teacher in Long Island, Lauren was living her dream when it happened, just like I was. My heart sank for her when she went viral. I read about her all over the place, including in an article in the *Guardian* where she explains how it all went down. A topless selfie she sent to her former boyfriend more than two years earlier surfaced. Her students were passing it around. She was fired. It's this quote she gives the *Guardian* that gets to me most: "It's one of those things you read about in the newspaper. You never expect it to be you." She's so right, no one thinks it can happen to them. Until it does. No one knows the profound devastation. Until it's them. According to that article, and most others written about Lauren's scandal, she has no idea how that picture—that sext—got leaked to become her *forever and for all to see*.

Sexting is defined and described differently depending on the source. Basically, it's the broad term given to the practice of sending nude, nearly nude, or sexually explicit photos or videos of one's self to someone else. It can also involve simply sexually explicit messages. It's getting more popular all the time, and studies show it is most prevalent in age groups ranging from preteens to middle-aged adults. According to a Pew Research study, one in five adults has taken part in sexting. Another study by JAMA reveals more than one in four teenagers has received a sext. Study after study shows the numbers are on the rise. So, what is the deal? Easy. It comes down to something so basic—human kind's fascination with sensuality. Wouldn't you say? Renditions of that fascination go back centuries. Think about Paleolithic art, and Renaissance masterpieces. The intrigue carries on into modern art masterpieces, and we can't forget Playboy, and even Playgirl magazines, and the like. Now, bring in our cell phone technology and it only makes sense our instinct and desire for titillation is going to take us to a proliferation of sexting.

It's so easy. It's so convenient. It can be so spontaneous. Some will say it's an empowering form of sexual expression, it's freeing, or maybe it's just having a little fun. Some attest that it can help fire up a new romance or even spark a new flame in an older romance. Bottom line, sexting is not going anywhere anytime soon. As much as that's a reality, so is the reality that sexting, especially with visuals, at any age is like playing with fire. A whole new level of temptation means a whole new level of danger.

\*\*\*

*Teen Sexting*

Let's talk about kids taking part, first. When it comes to anyone under eighteen-years-old sexting, there's no messing around. In most states it's illegal, period. That means it is illegal to take a picture, send a picture, possess a picture involving nudity or of a sexual nature involving anyone under the age of eighteen. Anyone who is caught taking part could ultimately face serious charges, which could mean serious penalties, including juvenile detention. While laws in each state vary, when sexting involves inappropriate images of a minor, even if they're exchanged between minors, it's often considered a form of child pornography. Child pornography is always a federal crime. That includes when the "child" is consenting, or even initiating. Teen sexting laws are changing regularly as it becomes more pervasive. You can easily find information on where your state is with underage sexting online. In fact, the Cyberbullying Research Center might have all the information you need in the "laws" section of its website. It explains sexting laws state by state.

While facing charges for teen sexting would be awful in itself, the virtual punishment could likely be much worse than what any judge could hand down. Yes, juvenile records are sealed, but we all know lips are not, and we all know what people are talking about is often what they're posting about and, again, scandal takes root.

Also, worth a quick mention. When sexting occurs between a juvenile and an adult (even when we're talking about people who are only a few months in age difference, like a seventeen and eighteen-year-old), the criminal aspect becomes that much more significant, as does the punishment.

*** 

## The "Viral-bility" Factor: How Sexting Can Go So Wrong

There's no way to know how any message or image you share via social media, text, or email is going to be received. No way to know how popular it could become, whether it's going to trend, in a good or bad way. In other words, what kind of "viral-bility" it might have. There's also no way to know where any message or image you share will end up, no matter how much it was intended for one person, and that one person only.

It doesn't take an expert to know that of all pictures or videos that get into the wrong hands, those involving nudity, near nudity, sexuality, or sensuality are going to spread first, and spread fast—fired off to unforeseen places and people. They blow the top off the "viral-bility" meter. It goes back to what makes sexting so tempting and intriguing in the first place, as mentioned earlier: human fascination. I say it often because it's worth repeating: You don't have to go viral on a global level for it to turn your life upside down. All you have to do is go viral in your own corner of the world for the humiliation to take a toll.

Remember that teacher, Lauren, whose topless selfie turned her life upside down? It's a classic case of a picture getting in the wrong hands. This is where I say too many things can go wrong on the human side. There are a number of potential scenarios. Here are three to consider:

1.  *I just shared it with one special person. It's no big deal.*

    Have you ever been told a secret and promised you wouldn't tell anyone else, but couldn't help telling just one more person? Who hasn't? I'm not saying no one can be trusted with a secret. I like to think most of us serve as trustworthy confidants, for the most part. Sometimes, though, you find yourself privy to that little something that's just too shocking, too heartbreaking, too scandalous, too juicy, whatever it is, that you just *have* to tell one more person. Maybe you just want to see if someone else's reaction matches yours, or want someone else's opinion or advice on this secret matter.

Who's to say that person you trusted with a secret picture, video, or message isn't going to share or show *just* their best friend, *just* that co-worker in the neighboring cubicle, maybe even *just* that stranger they start talking to on the treadmill next to them at the gym, or the like? They might not mean to violate you or even think about how crushed or betrayed you'd feel. They might not think of it as that big of a deal. When that one person shares, digitally or verbally, with *just one* more person we all know what happens next. The secret, *secretly* makes the rounds, the scandal erupts.

2.  *Lost/Stolen Phone*

"It was sheer panic, I felt betrayed, I felt paranoid, I felt alone." That's how Katelyn explains the feeling when nudes she sent to her ex-boyfriend made the rounds. If you recall from my mention of her in chapter two, it wasn't her ex's doing. It was the doing of the person who stole his phone, with the pictures Katelyn sent easily accessible. Apparently, just too tempting for the thief to not share with the world— with Katelyn's name attached. The thirty-two-year-old single mom was devastated, "I heard from a friend I was on the Internet somewhere, I go to the link they followed and, low and behold, it's my private photos."

The risk is certainly not limited to the phone or device where the material was received either. When you take a picture or video to send to someone else, or to share on social media, do you then delete it right away? I don't. In fact, it often ends up just sitting there in my gallery for months. I just forget about it. That's bound to happen with sexting images too. The device in which the images were taken getting into the wrong hands is just as much a possibility. That makes for another easy way for that material to be accessed and mass distributed.

A lost or stolen phone will always pose a significant risk for privacy violation. There is nothing securing our devices to us physically, at least not yet; there'll always be people who'll know how to hack into them.

Katelyn worked for months looking for ways to get the photos of her taken down, and even turned to the police for help.

**IAN ON IT:**

I bet police are often occupied with other things. The key is to make a report to memorialize the violation, and possibly setup a civil suit against the bad actor.

Seems the journey taught her a great deal. Perhaps most importantly, she told me, it leaves her with valuable insight into the soaring number of people who end up in a similar circumstance. With that, Katelyn Bowden started an advocacy group to help others navigate through such situations. It's called B.A.D.A.S.S. Army, which stands for Battling Against Demeaning and Abusive Selfie Sharing. She and other leaders in her group are making impressive strides in helping those who've been victimized reclaim their lives.

3.   *Revenge.*

Ugh. This is the worst. Who hasn't been in a relationship at some point in their life that went south? Somebody does somebody wrong, or there's just an awful fall out. Sometimes it's a relationship where a great deal of personal information was shared in confidence because, at the time, it sure felt like a forever bond. When that includes sexting, the vulnerability reaches new heights for the party who shared the private pictures. Sometimes that's both people.

Nude photos provide ammunition like no other when it comes to getting even with an ex-lover, or sometimes an ex-friend like that BFF who you shared too much with for kicks. They can be shared everywhere, and with everyone. That can include family and friends of the person in the pictures. It's called revenge porn, which, many agree, is an inaccurate term for it, when typically, the nature of the pictures is far from pornography. "Image abuse" is more like it. The humiliation resulting from image abuse ruins, even ends, lives. No one thinks this wonderful person they're in love with—well, at least crazy about—sure to be their "happily ever after" would EVER do something like that to them. It happens all the time, to people of all ages, in all sorts of situations, even married couples. Yes, adults who possess intimate pictures of their ex-spouse, or soon-to-be ex, are some of the worst offenders.

"He really did a number on me." That's what one Florida woman says after her ex-husband maligned her in a way most of us couldn't even fathom. Mary's case is an appalling example of revenge porn victimization. I met her in Pittsburgh a couple of years ago when I was asked to speak at a rally against image abuse. Mary was one of the victims taking part, marching for more stringent laws against it. A small, blonde, soft-spoken woman in her early fifties, whose pain was written all over her face. This kind of cause was the last thing this accountant and mother of teenagers ever imagined she'd be part of. When she shared her story with me, the humiliation she was suffering was palpable. Blindsided by scandal that was still so raw for her. I remember what that was like. It makes you feel like you'll never be the same again.

Mary was in the middle of a nasty divorce, when her soon to be ex-husband posted a topless picture of her. "My face and everything," she says. "The first time I saw it on the Internet, I almost passed out." That picture, she says, was a screenshot taken during a Skype call with her husband while he was overseas serving in the military, during the better times in their relationship. He asked to see her boobs during the call. She thought, *Why not?* and lifted up her shirt for him. Can you guess how she found out about the picture being shared? People started calling her, men who were intrigued by the photo. They got her phone number after her husband included all of her personal information when he uploaded the picture—hundreds of times. "He had me uploaded into chat rooms, porn websites, Craig's list dating, all these places. I had no clue." Making it worse, he made it appear as if *she* was the one posting the picture, proudly. It was enough to make her not want to leave her house, sure everyone in her small town saw it. Not to mention, she worried for her safety since her address was some of the personal information included in the posts.

Mary tried to press charges for cyber sexual harassment and stalking, but got nowhere. Too much red tape, too few people willing to help her, too little legislation on her side. It's an all too familiar story. After years of work, she thinks she got the photo taken off most of the sites. Still, she knows it's always going to be out there if someone really wants to find it, and thinks about how she might someday have to explain it to her grandchildren. Maybe a topless photo is no big deal to some people. But for Mary, the humiliation is life-changing. "I don't know if I'll ever really be able to trust anybody again."

\*\*\*

## Porn Site Potential

This is a risk few people ever think about when they're sexting. Remember how Mary mentioned her husband posted her nude photo on a number of sites, including porn sites? Remember Katelyn's pictures ended up on porn sites, too? Oh yeah, that's a big problem. There are what I call double and triple X-rated sites that have tech junkies working for them and, I would imagine, porn junkies. Their mission is to find pictures involving nudity. When they find them, whether they search for them, or someone like Mary's husband sends them their way, they post them on their sites A.S.A.P. along with any and all information they can find about the person in the photo. Age, where they live, what they do, you name it. When they have possession of that photo, good luck getting it off their site, or at least getting it off their site before those who subscribe to this culture, and then some, have their eyes all over it. Talk about violated. Talk about jeopardizing your hopes and dreams when that picture you trusted someone with ends up on, of all places, a porn site.

The goal of Katelyn Bowden's group, B.A.D.A.S.S., was originally to provide a support group for victims of image abuse, her mission also put her on a path to take on some of the most well-known porn sites. Sometimes she does it alone, as she's become quite the expert. Sometimes she recruits the help of other legal and technical experts. While she is forging a fantastic movement against these sites, each case (she deals with hundreds each year), is a battle. Each victim is a person who is traumatized, often in a very fragile state. But until her group, others like hers, and our lawmakers can criminalize image abuse on a federal level, the war has yet to be won and sexting makes for the perfect hunting ground for porn sites.

## IAN ON IT:

Forty-one U.S. states have Revenge Porn laws. Generally, they say that posting a nude photo of a victim with intent to cause emotional distress of the victim is a misdemeanor. If you are the victim of unauthorized posting of your nude photos, report it immediately to law enforcement!

The feeling of unwillingly having your name associated with that industry is hard to describe. I know due to the 2010 federal case of *Bosley vs. Flynt*. Yes, I sued Larry Flynt and his *Hustler Magazine*. The magazine, which got its start in the 1970s, is infamous for its pages of graphic hard-core porn. Flynt, the founder and publisher, infamous as well—known as the king of porn. Filthy rich and powerful.

A couple of years after I got copyrights to all the images from Key West, I got a phone call I'll never forget from a friend. "Catherine, I have to tell you something…" A friend of a friend of hers had seen my picture in *Hustler Magazine*. We contacted our lawyer. He did some research and indeed that was the case. Hustler held a contest asking readers to submit the name and picture of who they considered the "hottest news babe" in their town. Someone submitted my name and one of the photos that I acquired copyright ownership to.

Hustler's editors, who admitted in court they knew I owned the copyrights and never asked my permission to use the photo, still decided to send it to print. If I were to let it go, what message would I be sending? I worked too hard to get control of my life back and make it clear I wasn't going to back down and let anyone violate my copyrights. It ended in a week and half long federal court room jury trial against *Hustler Magazine*. Again, surreal. Again, another scandal I never saw coming. We won "David vs. Goliath" style. Our attorney, Andy Kabat, will forever be our hero. (You can read all about the courtroom drama—lots of it—in my forthcoming memoir, THE BARE FACTS.) What they did was downright wrong. It's just like what porn sites do to so many unsuspecting sexters. Taking even the slightest risk of becoming connected to porn in any way and against your will is never worth it. I'm sure I'm not alone in saying there are few associations that could cast a darker shadow on your *forever and for all to see*.

## YOUR SOCIAL MEDIA CHOICES: NOT JUST ABOUT YOU

When talking about pictures and posts you control, it's so important to keep in mind what you put out there, is not just about you. We are so uber-connected these days that what you post, your personal opinions, as well as your pictures, can easily be a reflection on others in your world. What you put out there, to some degree, can be perceived as representative of your family, your employer, your social circle, your school, your community, and more.

For instance, if you tweet out something that's insensitive or very politically incorrect, with your emotions getting the best of you, those in your world could certainly be left embarrassed by it, maybe even hurt when they're alienated by others because of their association with you. Consider this, a father tweets something obscene and it goes viral. Certainly, dad takes some heat, but the one who really suffers is his teenage son who is then taunted at school. Dad's audacious disregard becomes an indirect part of his son's identity that could be very difficult to live down in high school, and who knows how much further. I know of a case like this. The son was found dead in his bedroom not long after his dad's tweet became the talk of the town. It was determined to be a drug overdose. But of course, there was speculation that the embarrassment was enough to push the son over the edge.

There's also this to consider, it's getting more challenging, nearly impossible sometimes, to determine where your professional life ends and your personal life begins. Or vice-versa. With everything you post, like, share, and retweet saying something about you personally, inevitably there's the chance it'll reflect on your professional image as well. The line is blurred. Put yourself on the other side of this issue. Say you take your car to a certain repair shop because there's a mechanic there who does great work. You follow the repair shop on Facebook, so this mechanic came up as a friend suggestion some time ago and you added him. Then, suddenly, on your feed, you notice he puts out a shocking statement you find highly offensive and ignorant. Imagine it's something like expressing his support of racism, domestic violence or animal abuse. (I know, these are repulsive extremes—just making a point). It's his personal opinion and has nothing to do with his professional ability or his role as an employee for that shop. Now that you see this side of him, however, do you still want to associate with him?

So how do you avoid jeopardizing your working life when you turn to social media as just you? Have you heard the phrase, "Pause before you post?" It's so simple and can spare any of us a great deal of grief. Pause, look at the picture and take inventory. Pause, think about how those words might come back and haunt you, or affect someone else. Pause, to consider exactly *why* you want to like, forward or share that comment, picture, or video from someone else. Pause, if you're super emotional about something you want to express. Pause, if you've had alcohol. In fact, how about pausing until the next day in that case? In other words, don't engage in social media, or anything digital when you're drinking. Ever. When you're in control of which pictures and posts go out *forever and for all to see,* if they come back to haunt you, you only have yourself to blame. That kind of regret can be difficult to live with. If you rein in those impulsive tendencies more often, and instead, practice considering the bigger picture, which would be your hopes and dreams for the future, it's less likely you'll face that sickening question, *what was I thinking?* Self-discipline at its finest.

On so many levels, those pictures and posts you can control have the power to determine your *forever and for all to see.* Take control. There's no room for risk, especially when there are also those pictures and posts you *can't* control to think about.

# CHAPTER 4:

# PICTURES AND POSTS
# WE CANNOT CONTROL

"Social media gold." Have you heard the term? It's that content that brings a load of attention to your social media account, gets big likes, views, shares, comments, and gets you more followers, yay! It's the kind of content that goes viral, and is originated by you. Sounds good to a lot of people. Social media fame kind of stuff. A viral sensation. Like most everything, though, there's a downside. I'm talking about the horror of you becoming *someone else's* social media gold moment, when it's the last thing you expected.

## SURVEILLANCE CAMERAS

Think of your average day. You head out the door, stop for gas, maybe swing by a café to grab that cup of "please pick me up," then walk into your workplace or school. Maybe you go out to lunch, or run some errands during the day. After work or school, you go shopping, go to the gym, pick up kids from practice, go for a walk in your neighborhood, swing by the grocery store or grab some fast food, meet some friends out. On a day like that how many times do you think you are on camera? How about anywhere from fifty to seventy times? That's according to recent reports. If you find that surprising, you are not alone. Surveys show most people guess they make cameos fewer than five times a day.

"There's no privacy on the outside, once you leave your home," says veteran security expert Tim Dimoff. He should know. He spent twenty years in law enforcement, and twenty more in private security, running a high-profile company based in Akron, Ohio, called SACS Consulting & Investigative Services. As I walked the main street with him in downtown Akron, of course, there were those cameras you can see. But he also showed me how they're pointed at us from locations we can't see and don't even consider. We need surveillance cameras. They're meant for good, like deterring and helping solve crime.

Here's the problem. Have you ever had an embarrassing moment in public, like you tripped and fell, or realized your fly was wide open and just hoped no one saw it? Imagine you're at a gas station filling up and your skirt goes blowing up like crazy, a

Marilyn Monroe moment. Or, you're putting air in a tire, maybe changing a tire, not even thinking about that "moon" you're exposing. Now, imagine any of that being caught on security video. Clear, high quality video. You are now at the full mercy of the person in charge of that video. If he or she is scrolling through the footage and comes across something they think others would get a kick out of, or would give them social media gold, there's nothing to stop them from posting it. Even Dimoff agrees that the idea such video can be used by anyone for anything, for the most part, is a problem. When it happens in public it is fair game. "Everything has the ability to be abused until you define it clearly," he stresses. "You are inevitably going to see lawsuits filed claiming that releasing that footage did not serve the purpose of that camera."

Just a reminder to be mindful when you're out and about. Always assume that you are on camera.

## EVERYONE ELSE'S CAMERAS

We're minding our own business, just leaning up against a building on Honky Tonk Row in Nashville, taking it all in when we notice two young women walking toward us having a ball. They laugh, yell, stumble, flail their arms with animation. Both are clearly drunk. One seems much more so than the other.

"Hey, hey, y'all," the more intoxicated one yells, then starts singing at the top of her lungs while jumping up and down, with a few lewd gestures and profanity mixed in. Again, right in the middle of the crazy, busy sidewalk. For some reason the two decide to stop in front of us as if they've decided to visit us.

The less intoxicated one takes a place against the building next to my husband. "Where are you guys from?" she asks, striking up conversation full of energy we hope will rub off on us.

As we chat with her, we learn a few interesting things like where they're from, that they're sisters, and that they're in town for one of them to get certified as a personal trainer. We also find out this less drunk sister, who is charming while trying to stay composed, is a nurse. While we're chatting with her, the other one is practically knocking people off the sidewalk with her show.

Having a quick flashback to the "show" I put on in Key West and the scandalous nightmare that ensued, I turn to the less drunk sis. "Looks like you have your hands full…"

Before I could say another word, very drunk sis snaps at me, "Hey bitch…you only live once!"

Arm in arm, the two continue down the sidewalk. Becoming the center of attention of the crowd, a number of cell phone cameras are pointed right at them. What are those people going to do with the video and pictures they're taking? Heck yeah, they're going to post it all, giving their friends and followers a glimpse of the crazy fun time going on here in Nashville. What's to prevent those images from catching up to the women, especially now that there's facial recognition technology? Listen, I was fourteen-hundred miles away from home during my *you only live once* episode. There was no social media back then. Still, it hardly took ten months to catch up with me.

It doesn't have to be such a blatantly poor choice though. It doesn't have to be a college kid posting a photo with a bong, or a woman taking part in a wet T-shirt contest. Becoming the feature, or casualty, of someone else's social media gold can simply be that one time when your emotions get the best of you, especially in a public setting. Yes, this goes back to the idea that no one is immune to digital disaster, or social media scandal, no matter what age, gender, race or walk of life.

Not long ago a high-level female executive was not happy with her seat on a plane, next to a baby, and way in the back. She asked to be moved and when the flight attendant told her that wasn't possible, she had a fit, even threatening the flight attendant's job. Someone recorded the whole thing and posted the video on social media. It went viral. That executive was not only shamed like crazy online and humiliated, she lost her dream job, too. The video is part of her *forever and for all to see.*

So many people are walking around with their finger on the trigger of that cell phone camera. It's as if it's becoming an instinct to always be on the lookout to capture the perfect picture or video, the social media gold moment someone else might inadvertently hand over by way of their indiscretion or slip up. Have you ever noticed someone holding their cell phone at an angle that could put you in the camera crosshairs? Have you ever so discreetly taken a picture of someone else for any reason?

Who knew it would come to this? Who knew there'd be a day when everything you do, including every bad decision you make, every regrettable word you utter would have the potential to be representative of who you are? You can no longer presume that "What happens in Vegas, stays in Vegas," or Nashville, or Key West, or at the ballpark, at the bachelorette party, at the golf outing, or on your neighborhood street. What is meant for the moment is no longer guaranteed to stay in the moment when everyone has a device to document your every move. When so many crave social media gold, you can't be cautious enough. We do only live once, that intoxicated young woman we ran across in Nashville is right. Why take a chance on ruining that *once* with a silly decision to throw caution to the wind in such a high-profile and public way as she did. Especially when you know what you're doing is probably something you should not be doing, but temptation is getting the best of you, be mindful about what that moment might potentially look like in pictures or video.

While it's never been a good idea to let yourself get too carried away in public, now, it's a bad idea on steroids. Because we're human, there's always the chance of that happening though. It's one of those things we rarely see coming, obviously. It's usually a case of getting caught up in the moment. But when you do *feel* you might be in *that* mood, like you absolutely need to just let loose with some friends, how about a quick fix to keep it safe? Instead of a night of bar hopping, throw together a last-minute get-together, maybe a small impromptu-type party, or pity party, if that happens to be more like it, somewhere more private, with rules laid out regarding cell phone cameras. Maybe even no cell phones allowed at all.

# CHAPTER 5:

# YOUR WRITTEN WORDS

*What was supposed to be the most amazing day of my life—and career, turned into the worst. I will never forgive those responsible. **#REVENGE**.*

Just words, right? This is a Facebook post made by a man who was a TV news executive producer. A great producer, by the way. I worked with him early in his career and watched him flourish. I also worked with him when he put this unfortunate post out. Jaw-dropping, indeed. It was at the end of a long and exciting history making day in Cleveland sports. An NBA Championship parade and rally. All eyes were on Cleveland. It was an opportunity for those of us in the media to shine and show the world our potential. It was an opportunity for each of us in Cleveland TV news to potentially land Emmy nominations, including producers.

For the producer who wrote that post, however, unfortunate challenges arose that day that changed everything for him. Who knows whose fault it was that his newscast didn't go off as planned? So many things can go wrong that will have a producer pulling his or her hair out. Some of the most typical issues include reporter and videographer crews not being in place in time for live shots for some reason, blunders by the anchors or the control room staff, technical snafus, just to begin with. Who knows why he felt the need to lash out so publicly or why he chose those words in particular? None of that really matters. The decision he made that day to make that post, just words, cost him his dream job, his career. On a lower profile level, it was his scandal. As of writing this, he hasn't gotten another job in TV news, but I'm glad to say he has moved on to another career. It took some time, though.

We all know how overwhelming work frustration can be at times and how tempting it can be to lash out. So, I requested an interview with him hoping he could share how he came to terms with knowing impulse got the best of him. It had to require some soul searching. He declined the request, understandably. He is, however, the perfect example of how those *what was I thinking* moments with written words in the digital space can leave such an indelible mark on someone's image.

Words don't get the credit they deserve, when compared to images. But think about all they can do, really. They can lift you up, they can tear you down. They can inspire, intimidate, heal and harm. They can sabotage, and save. Incriminate and liberate. They can elicit empathy, or hurl hate. They can be magical or melancholy. Crafty or candid. The list is infinite. They're tools of expression that can be just as ambiguous as they are definitive.

One of the best feelings in the world is to know the words you chose were the right ones—words that opened doors for you, or better yet, made someone else smile. Then there's one of the worst feelings—having used word choices we regret. Sometimes you know you're going to regret your words *as you're saying them*, but can't stop yourself in time. Hate when that happens. Everyone has been in that circumstance when, if you could have one wish, it would be to take back what you just said. When it's the spoken word sometimes you wish you could take back *how* you said it, too. Verbal communication is so multi-dimensional. Tone of voice, inflection, pause and pace are just a few tools we use to paint our verbiage. Not to mention facial expressions.

With the written word, however, we don't have nearly as much at our disposal to make sure the reader knows *exactly* what we mean. It's pretty much word choice, punctuation, and emoji's—which do help somewhat. Also, with the written word, like the spoken word, once you hit post or send, it's back to the truth that there's really no way to "un-say" it. In the case of the producer, despite the fact the post was quickly deleted from his Facebook page, any attempt to take back his words would be futile. His regretful *forever and for all to see* took hold nearly immediately. It made news on TV industry websites, and the screenshot of it was circulating like crazy.

Arguably, one of the most infamous cases of "just words" on social media turning someone's life upside down is that of Justine Sacco. When I show audiences her 2013 Tweet, no matter what kind of speaking event I'm at, invariably there's a collective gasp.

*Going to Africa. Hope I don't get AIDS. Just kidding. I'm white!*

Who says something like that? Justine Sacco was thirty-years-old, living what appeared to be her dream life as a public relations executive. She was on her way to vacation in Cape Town, South Africa, when she posted that during a layover.

It went viral immediately, and the story would eventually top news headlines nationally. Full-blown scandal. Reports describe how she had no idea what happened until she arrived in Cape Town, turned on her cell phone and found her Twitter account blowing up. People were enraged, calling her names, slamming her with insults and threats. It's one of the stories featured in Jon Ronson's best seller, *So You've Been Publicly Shamed*. He writes about what some of the tweets said in response to hers, including this one, which resonates with me:

*Sorry @JustineSacco,* wrote one Twitter user, *your tweet lives on forever.*

What was she thinking? The same question so many had posed about my antics, *I* now also asked about her as I sat on the anchor set telling her story like so many other anchors told mine. It's the question the world was asking. Her answer—she was basically mocking such a preposterous idea by way of a sort of "joke," or "an outrageous commentary on the disproportionate AIDS crisis." Ronson explains that she alluded to the situation as crazy.

"'Only an insane person would think that white people don't get AIDS.' She told me."

Sacco was immediately fired and had to go into hiding for some time. She tells Ronson how even her family members were appalled and didn't understand her intention. While it took her some time, she was able to find employment again. Still, her Google search features her *forever and for all to see,* front and center. The power of words in our day of digital should never be underestimated.

One last note about "just words." How about that rush of heat that comes over you when you realize you sent an email or text to the wrong person? Or maybe, you inadvertently included others in that message who should not have seen it? How do you protect yourself when it comes to words? Like with a picture, always assume there's a chance everyone will see it. Know every message you put out there could potentially be documented for various purposes no matter who is at the receiving end—from your best friend to your boss. Choose your words and phrases carefully, be cautious about expressing harsh or insulting thoughts you might have about someone or something. The pause, pause, pause, before you post or send strategy certainly helps here, too. When possible, and especially when you're writing something where emotion is involved, it's a good idea to leave your message in a draft for a bit before sending it on. Often, when you revisit it, you'll see where you need to edit. Just think about the difference that one precautionary step might've made in the lives of Sacco and the producer. Hitting post or send when you're emotional can be just as dangerous as when you're inebriated.

As a journalist, I've discovered pausing can be quite beneficial on another level. I draft a story, a blog or an article contribution, feel okay about it, leave it for a day, an hour, maybe just a few minutes. When I go back to it, more often than not, I find the most unexpected slop—anything from a missing comma to a full-blown mischaracterization. It's as if that pause opens up space to see more clearly, to write with more acuity and purpose.

Oftentimes, we are especially in a hurry with our emails. Rush means risk. But one trick that's very helpful with some email services like Gmail, is using the delay option in sending your messages. It's amazing how helpful even a thirty second delay can be to avoid sending to the wrong person, or persons, or to stop the email altogether if you glance at your screen and notice something you don't like, like a stinking typo in an email, say, to your boss, or when you're applying for a job.

Rule of thumb with words: If it's digital, it's documentable. That section of the Miranda rights that reads *anything you say can and will be used against you…*can certainly be applied to what you say through a keyboard.

# CHAPTER 6:

# SHAMING & BULLYING

"I know what I can do. I'll take a picture of them and put it on Facebook. That'll teach 'em." It happens often. When we see someone doing something we disagree with, something we see as wrong, ignorant, or perhaps just laughable, it's so tempting to want to show the world by posting it on social media. That would be cyber-shaming. The excruciating effects of shame make it more powerful than most of us give it credit for. In fact, according to expert and author, Joseph Burgo, navigating shame is a "daily preoccupation" for most of us.

Shame has been used as a form of punishment throughout history. It's what the stocks and pillories were all about. Shame as punishment just takes on a different look today. A child gets time out in the corner of the classroom. A judge orders a thief to stand out in public with a sign admitting to and apologizing for his transgression. Ultimately, it's about coercing people to change their ways.

Then, there's the social media induced shame, which takes the persecution to a whole new level, allowing us to shame others in ways never before imagined. Worse, it goes beyond trying to get them to change. It opens a portal to lacerate others from every angle, just because we can.

The police officer I came across on my way to work not too long ago was ripe for the picking when it came to a potential tsunami of shame. I was working on the morning show at my Cleveland TV station, which meant I had to be on the road around three o'clock. Yes, three in the morning. Of course, I need my cup of joe to come to life. Like I did every morning, I pulled into the Dunkin' Donuts, placed my usual order, and as I pulled around the building to the drive-thru window, there was another car ahead of me. There's never another car at that hour, and this particular morning I happened to be running late. That car wasn't moving—a police cruiser, just sitting in the lane instead of moving ahead to the window where it should've been. There were no other cars in line. I had no time for whatever this was. I did not want to honk, not at a police officer, especially, even though the horn is made for such moments, right? Now, I know myself and I knew I was in no mood. I've been told I often wear my annoyance all over my face and my annoyance meter was about to peg. So, when I finally decided to slowly drive around the cruiser, I figured it would be best I didn't even look at the officer.

When I got to the window, I was greeted by my regular coffee lady. "What's going on back there?"

"I don't know." She shrugged. "His order has been sitting here for ten minutes. I'm not allowed to leave the building and I can't see anything from here. What do you see?"

I looked in my rearview mirror—oh, my goodness! There was the officer with his head slumped back and his mouth wide open. I jumped out of my car, rushed back to his and noticed his driver's side window was down and the car was still running. As I got closer, I could see him breathing. Shewww. Then, I heard it. A boisterous snort of the snoring sort. Yep, he was sleeping. A police officer asleep at a donut shop. Are you kidding me?

"Officer?" I said.

Nothing.

Then, again, a little louder, "Officer?"

His eyes opened, his head jerked up and he looked over at me with a range of emotions evolving over his face: shock, fear, embarrassment, gratitude, and finally, back to embarrassment.

"Are you okay?"

"Yeah, yeah, I'm okay," he responded slowly as he maneuvered to sit upright.

"Okay," I said, relieved and trying to refrain from chuckling. Walking back to my car I couldn't resist looking back to catch one more glimpse of the sleepy-eyed, boyish looking man in blue, and felt a need to bring some levity to the moment for him. "Remember this next time you pull me over," I joked.

He politely nodded his head and grinned. As I pulled off, it struck me just how lucky he really was that someone like me found him. Replaying it all in my head it's easy to see how tempting it might have been for someone to have taken a picture, or worse, video, of "snoozing cop at a donut shop" to share with the world online. For the person who shared that moment, it might've meant social media gold. Loads of likes, shares, retweets—a potentially viral moment! Not to mention, it would be the kind of material that makes it on the news.

At what cost to the officer though? I can't imagine the occupational violations there might be here. The evidence in one picture, or video clip, would have the power to turn that man's life upside down. Not only might it have cost him his job, maybe his career altogether, there's the inevitable personal humiliation and who knows what else? An avalanche. A scandal. It would be one of those scenarios of calling-out, or shaming someone else that makes me cringe. It comes down to a form of cyberbullying.

We don't always know the story behind what a situation appears to be on the surface. Maybe this officer had a sick spouse he'd been taking care of 24/7. Maybe he was dealing with some sort of disaster in his life that left him exhausted. Or, maybe he was just irresponsible. Who knows? Is it worth taking the chance and posting this moment, considering the price this officer—this man, husband, father, son, brother—might pay for the rest of his life? I give a resounding *no*.

The next morning, I drove through and asked my coffee lady what she found out when he finally pulled up to get his order. She said he explained he had a terrible cold and took the wrong cold medicine. Hopefully, it was enough of a wakeup call to make him go straight home. Out of curiosity, I did an informal survey of my co-workers about this situation and got a range of responses. Some agreed with me, that taking pictures and video would've been wrong, and would be really wrong to post. A few admitted they would've documented it in case something came up with that officer later. Some thought that moment, with or without pictures, needed to be brought to the attention of the officer's superior, and he needed to answer to it, but no need to share with the world. One woman, however, said she would've absolutely taken a picture and posted it. Her explanation was she felt he was wrong and he shouldn't have gotten away with it.

What about the possibility that others would see cruelty in you posting such images to shame the officer? Imagine how that would go over. That's how calling someone out online can back-fire. When people see you coming down on someone else, like humiliating that police officer, there's a likely chance they'll hurl back at you, perceiving *you* as a bully. As bad as the cyberbullying epidemic is, shoot, as bad as the bullying epidemic is altogether, there's also an adage that holds so true here. "What goes around comes around." Shamers get shamed. Once a bully is identified, they often become the target of harassment themselves. Just as harmful—the chance that the title of bully becomes part of their *forever and for all to see.*

Former model and actress, Dani Mathers, is a perfect example. Put briefly, she's accused of body shaming an older woman by secretly taking a photo of the unsuspecting lady in a gym locker room, then posting it with this caption: *If I can't unsee this then you can't either.* According to NPR, Mathers lost work, faced criminal charges and came under attack online. Despite her attempt to apologize, being a bully is a significant part of her *forever and for all to see.*

I remember one particular case of shaming gone bad, that was intended for good. A man, at his wits end with the poor service at a restaurant in his town, came up with what he apparently believed was a genius plan. He decided to go into the restaurant and place an order with his cell phone camera rolling. Indeed, he documented poor service. While still recording, he also let the person who waited on him, a young woman, have a piece of his mind. Then, he posted it. The idea was that it would get enough attention to where the restaurant would be forced to do better. It got attention, all right. The video went viral and the man came under attack for being a bully—a cyberbully. An intended good deed via cyber-shaming (oh, the irony) turned scandal. Not only did this man become the talk of the town, the taunting he took for that deed was enough that he had to up and move.

Then, of course, there's the purest form of cyberbullying where someone absolutely intends to hurt someone else, for whatever reason. I say it all the time: There's a different kind of torment when others poke fun at you, or attack you, when you see it playing out on a laptop or cell phone screen. It's as if the whole world is piling on—you are being stripped down and torn apart in front of everyone. I mean everyone.

I recall just running out to the grocery store and, even somewhat disguised with a ballcap and my hair pulled back, feeling like all the shoppers I passed by knew exactly what was going on with me and were in agreement that I was a disgrace and needed to be taken down. Since it continues online, day after day, one comment after another, one like, one share, one retweet after another, it permeates into your offline life, your real life. Seems it will never stop. Seems the attackers are right. Seems you deserve all you get. After all, it's all there in black and white. If you fixate on it enough, the reality gets grossly distorted and you truly don't know who you are anymore. It can be so bad, you don't even feel worthy of seeking help, too ashamed and embarrassed.

The devastating Rebecca Sedwick case is a perfect example, while also demonstrating the power of written words. The twelve-year-old Florida girl reportedly kept a journal in which she wrote:

*How many lives have to be lost until people realize words do matter?*

That entry was added shortly before she jumped off a concrete silo tower to her death in 2013. While she reportedly already suffered from depression, it's believed cyber-taunting was too much for her to take. The disturbing messages told her she was ugly and called her a "ho," but that's just the beginning. It's believed the taunting for her to commit suicide is where the words became lethal weapons. One allegedly told her to *drink bleach and die.* In an interview with CBS news, Rebecca's mother says this is the message she can't forget: *You haven't killed yourself yet… go jump off a building.* Chilling. Clearly, digital brainwashing at its worst.

"For the person who's been cyberbullied, that becomes their new reality," Michael Shelby explains, "a reality they become trapped in." The founder and director of the Technology Addiction Center, or TAC, in Connecticut specializes in helping people overcome a variety of technology or online related issues on the emotional/psychological side, and says what he sees when it comes to victims of online cruelty breaks his heart. "It's all they think about. They become scared, obsessed, very anxious. They feel trapped." He agrees with the characterization of it as brainwashing after witnessing victims become consumed by negative commentary to the point of eventually starting to believe it. Like Rebecca did. Like I did. Like more people do every day. Why is that? That's the puzzling question. His answer makes perfect sense, "It is a direct blow to their perception of self, of a certain self-image. This kicks at the foundation of that self-image. Makes us question ourselves, our reality. Very painful."

Adding to the potency, or intensity of cyberbullying, versus traditional in-person bullying, Shelby points out, is an ominous combination: anonymity and the opportunity for the bully to take their time to do their damage. It allows them to craft the perfectly worded virtual gut punch. Makes for what Shelby calls "a more exquisite brutality, a more exquisite viciousness."

It's hard to imagine someone taking pleasure in such barbarity. But experts like Shelby will tell you that's exactly what's happening—pleasure. For the rest of us, truly hurting someone else is never the intention. But here's something to keep in mind, blithely blasting someone else on a public platform—yes, even when you're just kidding around or believe you're harmlessly teasing—can do serious damage. You never know how that information, put out there for the world to see, might really affect them. It could hit them the wrong way on the wrong day and be that one thing that pushes them over the edge.

It's all about simply being kind online. There is one way to ensure you don't cause someone else unnecessary distress. One key word. Consent. Unless you're thoughtfully praising, complimenting, thanking, sending out a positive message about someone else, if you don't have their consent to post about them, don't do it. Consent is paramount on two levels. First, that person should be agreeable to you taking their picture or recording video of them. More importantly, it's crucial to get their consent to post, email, text, or in any way share any of that. If you can't get consent, that says everything about whether you should or shouldn't go for it.

You should be able to expect the same respect from others. Think about how often you agree to be in a fun group picture and once you see it—oh no—your eyes are closed, your bra strap is showing, your fly is open, your hair is a hot mess, or you're caught in mid-sentence with your mouth wide open. Isn't it a relief when the person who owns the picture, (remember, whoever takes the picture on their device technically is the copyright owner) agrees to delete and go for a redo? Basically, they're adhering to the consent principle. Why would you want to do anything different to someone else when it's a picture you take? Consent, consent, consent. Simple.

# CHAPTER 7:

# THE GOOD NEWS:

# REPUTATION RESCUE

I hope that a lot of what you've read in this book so far is eye-opening, or at least gives you a new perspective on our ever-evolving reality. Surely, it can be alarming, right? So much to think about, so much to look out for, so much that can go wrong. In a virtual split-second everything can change. I know!

As much as I'm all about raising awareness that it's *forever and for all to see*, as much as I'm about driving home the message that no one is immune, I'm also emphatic about the good news. Yep, the good news. This new brand of humiliation is, indeed, survivable. You do possess the power to rise above the anguish, as well as protect and redeem that all-important online reputation, which translates into reclaiming control of your all-important real life. While it only takes one electronic click to send it in a downward spiral, there's a lot more work that goes into the restoration and recovery. It calls to action a new mindfulness. It takes patience, strategy and time.

## TAKING CONTROL

Arguably, being armed with preventative measure options when we're aware of potential disaster or danger is priceless. We look for tools of all kinds to help us dodge risk in any way possible. How many passwords do you have in your digital world? I've lost count. Passwords are certainly tools we use in an attempt to protect ourselves. How about safety devices on dangerous items? Think of all that goes into child-proofing your home. We turn to gates, gadgets and gizmos galore. We also turn to all kinds of tools to make life easier, altogether. Look around your kitchen. Then, there's the garage.

We actually all have a special built-in tool to provide significant protection against online or social media scandal of all kinds. It activates automatically when you are in a variety of threatening situations. It tells you to stop when you're about to cross the street when that car is coming too fast. It tells you *no* when you're about to plunge into deep water and you're not a good swimmer. A life-saving tool! It's so simple. It's that little voice you have on the inside that tells you firmly when you should or shouldn't take action on a thought crossing your mind.

While you may listen to that voice most of the time, we all have moments when we choose not to and are somehow surprised how awful a situation turned out. Maybe you don't even know you're making that choice. Maybe that's because you're turning the volume of that voice down because you really *want* one more drink, even though the voice would tell you "Not a good idea." Or, how about you really *want* to pull that prank on someone, even though the voice would scream, "It could end so badly, not worth it." Or, you really *want* to flip the bird and scream out your car window to that driver who cut you off, even though the voice would tell you, "Don't be *that* person." Or, you really *want* to slam the door when you walk out of your boss's office because she didn't give you the raise or promotion you deserve. Your voice would say, "Keep cool, you could undermine your credibility and ruin future chances, too." Or, you are simply fed up with every-thing, and you *want* to shout out your frustration to the world on Facebook, even though the voice would tell you, "Relax, this will pass, and you'll be glad you didn't lose it online which could alienate a lot of people." (Yes, a reference to the former producer a few pages back.)

I promise if you leave the volume of that voice where it should be, engage that God given mechanism as often as you can, and just walk away from the temptation to do what you know you shouldn't do, you'll *never* regret that choice. Now, more than ever it's crucial to look within yourself, hear what your conscience is telling you, be the better person, the wiser person, the more cool-headed, reasonable, sensible person you truly are with every choice you make, online and off. Remember, you'll hear this from me often, there's so little room for that "*what was I thinking*" moment, online or off, before it could become attached to you *forever and for all to see*. With stakes like that, thank goodness for that precious tool you have, that little voice within you—always there to take care of you, if you let it.

Unfortunately, though, like so many other protections we have, that voice is not full-proof. While your good decision making can make a world of difference in keeping you on that path of greatness you're destined for, you are human. You're going to make a bad call here and there. Plus, you never know when you might become a target for this new brand of humiliation for no obvious reason. Pop-up scandal lurks around every corner in life. Since you picked up this book, maybe you've already freaked out a time or two about a picture or post you put out there, an image someone else put out there of you, a comment or information someone else shared about you without your consent. Maybe you're concerned for someone you care about who never hesitates to post pictures and videos. They see nothing wrong with mindlessly commenting, sharing, and retweeting, sometimes even while emotional or inebriated. (Did I mention yet that's the worst time to pick up your cell phone, for obvious reasons and for *anything* except a ride home? I think I did, but always worth repeating.) If you know someone like that, or, again, are worried about something you did, all this talk about *forever and for all to see* sure sounds like there's no going back. Enough to make you want to ease your sorrows in a package of Oreos, a weeklong Netflix binge in the same pair of pajamas or, of course, a bottle of wine. Wait a minute! Believe it or not, putting *forever and for all to see* in its place and rescuing your self-identity, self-worth, and your cyber-reputation is, indeed, doable.

Shewwww!

Take heart, says Adam Petrilli, the founder of NetReputation.com. In his nearly ten years at it he's seen a lot, "anyone can find themselves on the wrong side of online reputation information," he stresses, "but today, there are ways to fight back and take control of the situation." He explains by using technology against technology it's absolutely possible "to suppress and eliminate harmful information in a way that is effective and long-lasting." It's called online reputation management, or ORM. "Success in ORM," Petrilli says, "is based on a dual focus: technology that provides solutions, and knowing this is all about the tremendous impact it has on people and their lives." What he and his team do, he adds, is quite rewarding, especially considering how busy they are currently with tens of thousands of clients between all their offices at any one time. "Our company exists to give the underdog a fair and fighting chance in a world where malicious online behavior is more often the norm than the exception, where too often one piece of information can be unfairly exaggerated or misinterpreted and takes on a life of its own." That a business like NetReputation thrives says all we need to know about the digital intrusion on our society, and it's potential to scandalize. On the other hand, that companies like this are so busy also serves as proof there is a fix. Takes more tools.

When it comes to an assault on your integrity online, experts have varying thoughts on how to deal with it initially, that is, before it gets to the point that you need an ORM company for help. Every case is different, but the first thing you want to have happen is to stop the smearing, stop others from disseminating any content that will damage your online image. A Pew Research study indicates most people do exactly what I would most strongly advise—they don't respond to those who join in on the campaign to hurt them. It adheres to the notion of "don't feed the trolls" which means the less attention you give them, the more likely they are to die off. That's one tool.

Next up—acknowledgement. You deal with the matter directly by briefly addressing it without using or inciting emotion. "If you become the target of rumors or misinformation, then fight back with facts," Marie Ennis-O'Connor, a communications strategist explains. "If you make a mistake, then admit it and show how you will fix the mistake." That can be a wise choice as well, whether you're dealing with cruelty, humiliation, or accusations as an individual or a business. But she stresses this shouldn't apply to those who persist in hurting you. In that case, it's back to "don't feed the trolls."

My experience put me face to face with this dilemma in my original attempt to stop the picture and video spread, and stop the cruel comments. Ignore or acknowledge. Both strategies were worth a try. First, I very publicly took responsibility, fessed up to my indiscretion, expressed my disappointment in myself and my remorse. I even apologized. Why apologize? People ask me that all the time. After all, I didn't hurt anyone or do anything illegal. I get that. However, I did let down many who expected more of me, at least better judgement. Not to mention, my escapade ended up causing others grief. My family and friends were caught in the middle, left burdened with defending me and helping me through it. Then, of course, I know my lapse of judgement, or—call it like it is—my stupidity, failed a lot of people, including my employer who trusted me to maintain integrity, my co-workers, and my viewers. All of those people were affected by what I did. I am truly sorry.

Sincerity, authenticity, and vulnerability are key if you go this way. In retrospect, brevity is important too. No reason to drone on with an apology that leaves more room for misinterpretation and more attack. My decision to acknowledge the scandal, versus ignore it, helped. Kind of. At least for a minute. It's not as easy to continue attacking someone after that person surrenders. Not as invigorating, I would imagine. That allowed for a brief lull in the mean-spirited comments, with the supporters surfacing like crazy, enough to blunt the haters, for which I will forever be grateful.

Soon, though, the die-hard haters were back at it, full-force, mostly strangers. This time using my acknowledgement of my poor choice against me. Seems my in-depth, and again, very public explanation and apology provided fodder to those on a mission to bring me down. As miserable as that chapter in my story was, I don't think I could've done it another way. I had to address it head on. After that, however, I chose to and was strongly encouraged to avoid engaging with haters online. I'm talking NEVER, under any circumstance, no matter what they said to elicit a response. In hindsight, I don't think I had the strength to indulge them anyway. Also, now I see how it would've been a sure-fire way to spike the momentum of an online campaign determined to bring me to my knees.

## Carson King: A Case Study

Twenty-four-year-old Carson King chose the acknowledgement route too, regarding racist tweets from when he was sixteen. The Iowa man's public apology read, *I am embarrassed and stunned to reflect on what I thought was funny when I was sixteen years old.* He extended that apology in a TV press conference. His was a case of instant fame turning to infamy in a matter of only a few days.

It all started when King held up a sign at a college football game reading *Busch Light Supply Needs Replenished.* The sign also gave information to his Venmo account to donate to his beer fund. A joke, he called it. The joke made it in front of an ESPN camera—network TV. Money poured in! Thousands of dollars, reportedly, and suddenly it appears King's dream was born, to fundraise for charity. When he announced he was donating the money to the local children's hospital, Anheuser-Busch and Venmo jumped in quickly offering to match the donations. Other corporations donated to reportedly bring the donation to more than a million dollars. Yes! King was a hero, making the rounds on national talk shows to express his gratitude and excitement. His *forever and for all to see* was taking shape in the best possible way.

Then, the infamy. A newspaper reporter dug up the racist tweets from years ago. Again, King made national news. He was shunned and shamed. Some of the big companies, while announcing they'll keep their commitment to help children, denounced King and immediately went public in cutting ties with him. That includes Anheuser-Busch, which even created a beer can hailing King before knowledge of the tweets. His recently amazing *forever and for all to see* was under attack—about to become legendary in all the wrong ways. National scandal.

King had a choice. He could've faded off in silence with his head hanging low, or accept responsibility. His apology went on to say, *I cannot go back and change what I posted when I was a sixteen-year-old. I can apologize and work to improve every day and make a meaningful difference in people's lives.*

Of course, he would have no idea how that would go, but clearly something inside him told him that's what he needed to do, regardless, while also expressing hopes of continuing to raise money for the hospital.

I would imagine King received plenty of hate backlash online for those tweets from years ago. But what happened after his apology serves as more proof recovery is possible. People flocked to his defense, campaigned against Anheuser-Busch and the newspaper where the tweets were dredged up. Ironically, the reporter who did that deed was fired for allegedly having questionable tweets in his past, too. The best part is, according to King's current website, the money kept coming in—a total of three million dollars. Also worth noting, another beer company stepped up to celebrate King's authenticity and generosity. Geneseo put out a letter on social media accepting King's public apology and acknowledging his growth with the "noble act" of donating his beer money in the first place. They also announced they were tapping a new brew called "Iowa Legend" with a portion of the sales going to King's charitable effort.

It looks like he's still rising above. As the founder of The Carson Foundation (TheCarsonFoundation.org), he's captured his dream, of "helping families and children in times of need and uniting communities to make a difference," as it's eloquently spelled out on his homepage.

***

The choice of which tool to use to take back control of your life, online and off—acknowledgement or silence, should never be a knee-jerk reaction. It needs to be well thought out. I would recommend the good old pros versus cons write out and discussion with those you trust, while sorting through your emotions. A plan on how to handle your situation, no matter what you choose, is the first step to recover and put that *forever and for all to see* in perspective, just as someone like Carson King did.

## MOVING ON

No matter how you respond to an online nightmare, drama or scandal, the next step is knowing how to put it behind you. This is where experts who work for a company like NetReputation.com can provide a lot of guidance. "We are people too, and can relate to making mistakes, and having regrets," Adam Petrilli says. "We also know how it feels to be treated unfairly. We should all be able to, and have the right to move on from those moments." Amen!

To counter online permanency—to perhaps mitigate a damaging *forever and for all to see*—he offers three steps to make moving on a reality.

1.  **Search yourself.** Have you ever Googled your name or the name of your business or organization? Not everyone thinks to do that. Whether or not you are dealing with an issue, Petrilli stresses it's always good to check in on that online image once in a while. "You don't always know when others posted something about you, or shared a photo or video capturing you in a bad light. That can be especially disconcerting and needs addressed. Sometimes people later find out a screen shot of one of their own posts, even texts or emails they thought was private generated unexpected negative attention years ago." That goes hand in hand with the notion that no one is immune, right?

2.  **Delete, Delete, Delete.** That would be a logical step. Delete what you can as far as pictures, posts, video, comments, emails, and texts that show you in anything other than a good light. You might also need to ask others to delete items about you that have the smallest potential to come back and haunt. In some cases, that's not as easy as it sounds, especially when it's *someone else's* inconsiderate or insidious digital deeds that got you in a mess. As far as that goes, maybe a letter from an attorney to the offender would make all the difference.

**IAN ON IT:**

Cease & desist letters from an attorney skilled in online matters and social media may cause the poster to stop for fear of being in trouble with law enforcement or being sued in a civil action.

3.  **Populate with positive**. Through the response I get when I mention this at my speaking events, it's become clear this step is not so well-known, but could be the most valuable step in overcoming an objectionable *forever and for all to see*. For every picture, post, comment that you delete, replace it with content you want people to know about you, to say about you, to see about you. I suggest, as a rule of thumb to staying disciplined in this mission, putting out five to ten new pieces of content for every one you delete.

    "A comprehensive approach," Petrilli calls it. It's about creating positive content to counteract the negative—a proven way to get results especially when you create attention grabbing content across several platforms. That can mean taking your campaign past social media and considering creating a blog show-casing your wisdom, compassion, strength and the rest of the great things the world should know about you. How about creating your own website? More individuals are finding that quite helpful, especially if they're in the job market. For a business or organization, a website is a "must" for ramping up business as well as maintaining a strong, positive online image. Experts suggest hiring web designers who know how to strategically place it online with powerful SEO, search engine optimization.

While anyone can start to repair their online reputation by focusing on populating with positive, Petrilli and his team take it to the next level for their clients through "sophisticated review management and content development and distribution." Sounds complicated, but it comes down to experts doing advanced research to determine exactly how to get the new content to rank higher in search engine results than the damaging information. Something I found quite interesting especially for companies and organizations is the idea of using this strategy proactively—creating so much positive buzz that when/if negative information does surface it has less of a chance to put a dent in an organization's reputation. Populating with positive is a great way to be vigilant.

Remember, no matter how many times you delete, the likelihood of it really disappearing is slim. So, simply put, the goal of this step is to push the unwanted content out as far as possible into cyberspace, which translates into pushing it out further in your Google search. If it works, the unwanted material won't appear until page twenty, or thirty or beyond.

Who actually goes past a page or two when they've done a search? We're usually satisfied with the first couple of pages. Ideally then, if you keep populating with enough positives, those first several pages when someone searches your name will make you shine as you should.

# CHAPTER 8:

# *PACT* PAST IT

There's more to getting past it than rescuing your reputation. Sometimes, much more. The emotional recovery is just as crucial, if not more so. Research shows the effects of any sort of bullying during childhood can linger well into adulthood. In fact, a recent study indicates the existence of PTSD (post-traumatic stress disorder) in victims of cyberbullying. The authors of the study, published in the BMJ Journals: Archives of Disease in Childhood, surveyed more than 2200 students and found approximately 35 percent of those who reported involvement in cyberbullying demonstrated "clinically significant" symptoms of post-traumatic stress. While there is plenty of reason to focus on the damage it can do to kids, who's to say it's much different with adults? That's something to consider when research shows cyberbullying among adults is skyrocketing, especially among those in their twenties and thirties. Some of the most eye-opening infor-mation comes from a Pew Research Center study. It reveals nearly four in ten American adults personally experienced harassing or abusive behavior online.

Of course, the emotional trauma is somewhat different for everyone, but what I experienced and what I hear others talk about most is the hopelessness that sets in, maybe too hopeless to even attempt something like reputation recovery. Maybe you'd think what's the point in even going on? The pain can blind you to any consideration that there could be, rather, there IS life after online/ social media cruelty, shame, humiliation, or embarrassment. My friend, I'm living proof it is survivable. Really survivable. If I can do it—you can do it!

In recalling how I found my way through those dark times, to finally see once again the light life offers, I've come up with what I call the PACT strategy. It means making a pact with yourself, for yourself, and for those who love you, to not give up, and keep pushing your way through to the other side of the torment. It calls for patience, first, and belief that it works, second. Again, I'm proof that it works. The commitment is made on four simple levels:

*P* - *People*

*A* - *Abandon*

*C* - *Connect*

*T* - *This too shall pass.*

## *PEOPLE*

We are here for each other, to enjoy each other, to listen to each other, to comfort each other, to guide and support each other, to challenge each other, to celebrate with each other, to grieve with each other. There's no end to the list of how we're here for one another. What would we be without each other? If someone you cared about was suffering in any way, wouldn't you want to know about it? Wouldn't you want to help them in any way you could? Wouldn't you feel bad if they kept it to themselves and agonized alone?

When you're experiencing the kind of uncertainty and emotion triggered by online/social media cruelty or drama, the first thing you should do is talk about it with someone you trust. The last thing you should do is keep it to yourself. Dr. Barton Goldsmith puts it beautifully in *Psychology Today: When you express how you really feel (in an appropriate manner), problems get solved, relationship issues get resolved, and life is easier. In addition, you will like your life better because you're not holding on to unhealed or confusing feelings.*

Sure, explaining what's happening in your cyber-world to those in your real world might be uncomfortable, even embarrassing, then there's the concern it could make it all worse somehow. It's not even uncommon to feel that it's all your fault, right? I sure had that going. That could make anyone more inclined to hide, which can include anything from shrouding the situation by staying quiet about it, to alienating yourself from family, friends and the rest of the world out of shame. All while continuing to watch the attack play out online in isolation. By the way, isolation is used as a form of punishment, you know. Solitary confinement. Aren't you already being punished enough?

Dr. Tamar Blank, Director of Riverdale Psychology in New York, sees patients who deal with issues like bullying regularly. She's passionate about turning to your people for support. "When you don't tell other people, it's like holding a weight; it feels heavier to carry alone." She also stresses the value of letting others field the information about what's taking place to allow a more objective perspective.

I consider it activating your army. My army is made up of my faith, family, and friends. When I'm in trouble, or just troubled, in any way, I need all three parts of my army. Who makes up *your* army? It doesn't have to be big, maybe yours is that one person who is especially important in your life. That one person can make all the difference, perhaps even a life-saving difference. Just like you expect them to trust you to help them through their tough times, they expect the same from you. Don't let them down.

### *ABANDON*

Get away from the source of your suffering. That means shut down the social media account where the cruelty is coming from. Maybe that means getting off all social media—for the time being, at least. If you can't quite do that, Dr. Blank suggests it might be a good time to simply turn your social media over to one of your people to keep an eye on the situation for you.

The more you dwell on the cruelty or harassment, the more it's going to suck you in and the worse it's going to seem. A sort of brainwashing power, as mentioned previously. Especially with the most nocuous comments, there's often a compulsion to look further to see who exactly is joining in. Some people you might know, others are strangers who might know people you know, who think it's cool to be part of something trending that they have no clue about. Suddenly, you internalize and start believing the awful things being said even by people who never met you.

Ever wonder why we tend to focus on the negatives, and sometimes dismiss the positives, especially with comments about us? For instance, an overweight person loses a bunch of weight. Family and friends are super impressed, commenting on that person's improved energy, how much younger and happier they look. Then, there's that one person who says something stupid like how their clothes look awful on them now, or they don't think of them as the same person anymore, or how their face looks gaunt. What type of comments are going to be the loudest to that person who finally hit their weight loss goal?

There were days I'd get off the anchor desk after what I felt was such a good newscast I wanted to high-five myself. No stumbles, strong delivery, substantive or witty chit-chat with my co-anchor, exceptionally engaged and energetic throughout the 3½ hours. Not that easy to accomplish. Even more challenging for me has always been finding that "nailed it" feeling. Then, it would be time to correspond with viewers via social media or email. While there'd be lots of great correspondence, it would only take that one negative comment to ruin my high. It could be something as insignificant as "your hair looked bad today," or you "mispronounced that man's name, what's wrong with you?" The more seasoned I became, sure, the more it would roll off my back, but those comments always got my attention.

"We tend to focus on that which is negative in order to protect ourselves," says Dr. Blank. She explains that human tendency, in particular, comes from an adaptive evolutionary place. In other words, it's a subconscious awareness that anything negative has the potential to cause harm, and "we're in constant motion of how do I protect myself."

Perhaps that's part of why we quickly find and obsess over negative comments about ourselves online, while glossing over the positives. The negative is signaling alarm, and of course, when you know where there's a source of potential harm, you don't want to take your eyes off it. Dr. Blank says recognizing a source of harm is one thing, obsessing over it is another and can do its own kind of damage.

Here's the reality: That small percentage of small-minded people sounding off on you online is absolutely insignificant. They probably didn't give any thought to that "like" they gave to a mean-spirited post about your new hairstyle, for example. They just click and move on. Others who take part, or even start the campaign, could very well be acting out on issues they have with themselves according to most experts and study after study. What they're throwing out at you might be nothing compared to the misery or insecurity they're experiencing. But for some sad reason taking to social media, messaging or emailing about someone else makes them feel better about their own situation. Why give any of that any of your time or thought?

Close shop. Get back into the real world of family and friends and doing those things offline that are comfortable, familiar and enjoyable. Refocus on the things that matter—that help you progress, instead of dwelling on nonsense that will only hold you back. Explore a new hobby, a new sport, spend more time with your dog, with your kids, with your parents, catch a movie—just stay away from the unnecessary screen time. *No good will come from it.*

It's similar to when a social circle, a clique, turns hurtful. For the most part, you can't change the mean momentum. The more you pay attention to it and respond to it, the more you fuel it, but worse, the more you are choosing to allow it to affect you. Abandoning a source of angst is not only a healthy choice, it can also be super empowering.

## *CONNECT*

Connect with professionals who can help you. Like myself! Like those you'll find on the many anti-bullying websites—just Google it. There's quite an effort underway to stop online cruelty, I applaud that, certainly. Truth is, though, purposeful embarrassment, harassment, humiliation, AKA, bullying, has been around since the beginning of mankind. Strangely, it's part of human nature for some to different degrees. While today's effort to stop the cruelty has got to be putting a dent in it, we all know it's not going to bring an end to it. The good news is just as the movement to *stop* bullying is underway—especially cyberbullying—there's also a growing number of resources to help those who already find themselves targets, or victims, rise above.

There are so many people, of all ages and from all walks of life, who are going through the same thing. Cyberbullying. org has a whole section where people who've encountered some degree of digital drama share their experiences, from being poked fun of, to full out social media scandal. Whether you did something which inadvertently sparked a firestorm, like I did, or you just happen to be a random target of cyber-humiliation, shaming or bullying, there's an increasing number of professionals trained to help. There are people who know how to guide you through it. They see it every day. All kinds of stories. All levels of help-lessness and hopelessness, guilt and defeat. On the emotional or psychological level, you can find counselors and therapists online or in your own community. You can find other victims who've made it through and want to help you in online support groups. One of my favorites is iHeartMob.org, where you essentially have cheerleaders standing by. Most of the top anti-bullying websites provide that kind of support as well. (Please see the resources section in the back of the book for a list of sites.)

Other ways to connect your way to the other side of digital cruelty might include reaching out to an attorney or going straight to law enforcement. Cyberbullying isn't just about hurting someone's feelings, it can be a crime depending on which state you live in and the degree of harassment. We're talking a jail time crime. There are laws to protect you when things get out of control, which can happen with just one post, email, or text that crosses the line. For a better idea, Stompoutbullying.org includes the following in its list of when cyberbullying can become a crime:

- Harass someone especially if the harassment is based on gender or racism
- Make violent threats
- Make death threats
- Make obscene and harassing phone calls and texts
- Sexting

**IAN ON IT:**

Cyberbullying becomes a crime when someone (1) posts personal information about a victim or (2) posts a message harassing the victim with intent to cause the victim to reasonably fear for his or her safety. If you are a victim of cyberbullying, do not hesitate to make a police report. Law enforcement could assist you STOPPING the bullying, and/or you could recover for the harm caused to you in a civil lawsuit against the cyberbully.

Reach out. Open arms are there for you today.

## THIS TOO SHALL PASS

Bet you've heard this before. It's my favorite part of the pact. The phrase apparently originated in the nineteenth century and is, of course, used widely. It was even used in a famous speech by good ole Abe Lincoln. Until I went through my situation I never paid much attention to the phrase. Now, it means the world to me. I live by it. It's my deepest hope that you'll integrate it more into your life as well.

How many times have you gone through something in your life, no matter how old you are, and thought, *This is the end of me, I'll never outlive this*? And what happened? You're here! You made it. Now, when you reflect on those moments, you might think, *What was the big deal?* That's because something else happened you might not have contemplated. With each tumultuous event, you develop skills that make the next one less challenging to navigate. Those past life events start to seem insignificant because each of them makes you stronger, makes you wiser, and makes you more equipped and on standby to help others who find themselves in similar circumstances. Right? That means each of your struggles plays a *significant* role in making you the wonderful you that you are!

Once my drama decade came to a close and I stepped out of survival mode, introspection kicked in. From major health issues to global humiliation, I started to understand everything passes, and, God willing, life goes on. Sometimes it's not quite the same life you knew, maybe for a bit it's not as comfortable as what you used to know. That's okay, even more than okay. You know why? Because it has to be. Life changes can sometimes be uncomfortable, but they'll always bring about growth. In nature, when there's no change, growth gives way to decay.

While the *passing* part of *this too shall pass* is based on the idea of putting something behind you, don't lose sight of the fact that what's behind you serves as your pedestal. It sets you up, builds you up, to do better with what's to come. It's up to you to make sure each "this too shall pass" moment counts, just as it's up to you to make those good moments count, too. Life is chock full of character building, learning moments—enriching opportunities. What we learn counts not just for us. It counts as well for those who come through our lives, whether we're talking friends and family members or strangers you strike up a conversation with on the train or in the doctor's waiting room. You never know when the information you acquire, through good times or bad, can help someone else. Make it count to do something good in this world. The last thing you want to do is let those learning moments, especially the rough ones, go down in vain and not be put to use somehow, for someone. That transformation of a *this too shall pass* moment to a *making it count* mission is beyond precious. It's victory in its purest form.

# CHAPTER 9:

# CAPTURE YOUR DREAMS,

# SCANDAL FREE

What is your dream for your life right now? What do you want to see happen in your future? Your near future. Your far future. You might remember earlier I talked about my dream of working in TV news—a dream I had for my life since I was young. Maybe your dream, like mine, is connected to a career you envision—a passion you just have to pursue. Maybe it's to make it to the next level in the career path you're already on. How about starting a charity that improves the lives of millions, or finally launching your own business that lets you put your talents to work like never before? Or, is it more on a personal level, like finding that special someone, or having a family of your own?

Our hopes and dreams often take a few turns throughout life. As we get older, more of us dream about the happiness and success of our children, financial freedom, a peaceful retirement, or even an exciting and adventurous retirement. You might dream of becoming free of something that's holding you back. How about this one—the dream to just have your life stay on the very track it's on, where all is good?

The best thing about dreams—the sky's the limit! Now, I'm blessed with getting to live another dream too, using my story to make a difference.

While we all have our big goals, sometimes we get so entrenched in the rigors of everyday life that we aren't so conscious of really having what we'd call a dream, exactly. I so get it—the *just getting by* thing. That's when I say ask yourself what is it that gets you out of bed every morning. If you truly think about it, it's *more* than simply doing what you need to do, all that routine stuff. I bet you'll realize it's about tackling one more day to get one step closer to what you want ultimately—your dream. No one ever said capturing a dream is easy. I'll bet, though, you've put more work into reaching that goal than you give yourself credit for AND are closer to it than you realize.

There are certainly stumbling blocks beyond the just getting by rut. Hell, life happens. Moments we never saw coming can certainly jolt us off track, like job or relationship loss, family issues, and certainly social media scandal. I like to look at most of those problems as life's detours with some scenic routes (not *always* pleasant scenery). They're invariably distracting—similar to what you feel when you come across a DETOUR AHEAD sign in your travels, literally. You're on your way with a destination in mind, when you have to throw on the brakes. When you think about it, a detour while you're driving is guiding you around or away from some sort of potentially serious issue: a roadway that's crumbling, an electrical line or tree down, an accident or construction that will make you come to a full stop for hours. There's more to consider than the immediate inconvenience. How about the possibility the detour helped you avoid a real disaster? In that respect, life's detours, while they might slow us down temporarily, can potentially guide us to a better route, shake us up a bit to open our eyes to a different perspective. That could include knowledge we didn't know we needed to make a dream a reality. A detour, or distraction, might even be the source of an epiphany which redirects you to a new and improved dream that you never considered.

Accepting and finding the value in a detour is a choice, as opposed to letting it turn into anger, or hopelessness. But, even when there's no real detour, how you steer through all the other twists and turns on your journey counts too. Every choice we make counts in the journey to claim our dreams. Bad choices will happen, but just as one bad choice can derail, a good choice can empower and even turn the worst of things around. Each kind of choice can offset the other, which makes the decision to never give up *the choice* that will eventually get you where you want to be—living your dream.

It goes back to using that little voice within that tells you when you shouldn't do something, your built-in decision-making tool. That used to mean easy choices like don't break the law, don't cheat, don't be reckless with your driving or do anything too dangerous. Don't burn bridges with others or show disrespect. Some pretty clear cut, easy to follow guidelines that come down to common sense and courtesy.

Today, though, a whole new set of guidelines comes into play. Seems the user's manual to navigating toward your dream is being rewritten continuously, each time raising the bar on our decision-making skills. The faster our technology advances, the quicker the rewrites. Each new edition calls for a new dimension of mindfulness. For instance, adding a simple "like" to a post seemed harmless not long ago. Today, that one "like" can say many things about you that you never thought of, intimations about your agenda, your character, that can uproot your plan. Used to be you could make the human faux pas of raising your voice at someone in public, maybe your spouse, your kid, your friend, maybe the drive-thru worker who can't get your order right. With remorse setting in immediately, you'd apologize and would expect to move on. You *should* be able to do that without fear of long-term consequences because no one is perfect. You'd put that *what was I thinking* moment behind you, learn from it and hopefully be less inclined to do it again. Now, that momentary lapse in judgement when your emotions get the best of you could haunt you *forever and for all to see* when someone captures it on their cell phone camera and posts it.

Bottom line, our dreams are at risk like they've never been before if we don't adjust and aspire to harmonize with the high paced transformation that comes with advancing tech. Technology is engineered to help us, but it's up to us to make sure it does just that, not the opposite. Up to us. Yes, kind of overwhelming.

Most alarming though—the idea that any of us living, breathing, God-made masterpieces would give in to letting a cold, unfeeling, digital contrivance get in the way of what we truly want for our lives.

Online cruelty, cyberbullying, shaming, humiliation—all of it—it is scary. It's real. The danger of falling victim is omnipresent. No one is an exception. But just like *every* danger we're up against, the more we're aware of it, the more we're vigilant about it—the less likely we are to fall victim. In addition, the more we listen to that little voice inside warning us of risks, and guiding us toward wiser choices, the more likely we are to go ahead and capture those dreams, uninterrupted. A life scandal free. As it should be.

Keep dreaming!

# SOURCES

## INTRODUCTION: WHO AM I TO TELL YOU? GREAT QUESTION

Linda M. Linonis, "Bosley has arrived as "it" girl of searches."
*The Vindicator*, Youngstown, Ohio, February 2004

Emily A. Vogels, "The State of Online Harassment," Pew Research Center, January 13, 2021; https://www.pewresearch.org/internet/2021/01/13/the-state-of-online-harassment/

Kirsten Weir, "Worrying trends in U.S. suicide rates," American Psychological Association, March 2019; https://www.apa.org/monitor/2019/03/trends-suicide

## CHAPTER 1: MY STORY, ABBREVIATED

David Letterman's Top Ten List: The 10 Best Things About Having a Stripper as an Anchor, January 23, 2004; http://www.oocities.org/jaylipp/Letterman/topten04.html

Catherine Bosley, "My Naked Nightmare: A Lesson in Surviving Humiliation," TEDx Talk, December 2018, https://www.ted.com/talks/catherine_bosley_my_naked_nightmare_a_lesson_in_surviving_humiliation

Emily Bazelon, "May Joe Francis of *Girls Gone Wild* Rot in Jail," *Slate*, May 8, 2013; https://slate.com/human-interest/2013/05/girls-gone-wild-founder-joe-francis-will-go-to-prison-and-he-deserves-it.html

Kelly Phillips Erb, "Lawsuits Gone Wild: Francis Still Fighting Back Against Foreclosure," *Forbes*, May 23, 2016; https://www.forbes.com/sites/kellyphillipserb/2016/05/23/lawsuits-gone-wild-francis-still-fighting-back-against-foreclosure/?sh=3617f0dd73b1

Claire Hoffman, "From the Archives: Joe Francis: 'Baby, give me a kiss," *The Los Angeles Times*, August 6, 2006; https://www.latimes.com/style/la-tm-gonewild32aug06-story.html

Gene Marks, "10 Mysteries About the Girls Gone Wild Bankruptcy," *Huffington Post*, March 8, 2013; https://www.huffpost.com/entry/girls-gone-wild-bankruptcy_b_2836314

## CHAPTER 2: MYTH: THERE'S PRIVACY ONLINE

Catherine Bosley interview with Richard Storrs, Attorney, The Storrs Law Firm, Atlanta, GA, March 30, 2020; https://www.storrslaw.com/attorneys/richard-storrs/

Dave Lewis, "iCloud Data Breach: Hacking and Celebrity Photos," *Forbes*, September 2014; https://www.forbes.com/sites/davelewis/2014/09/02/icloud-data-breach-hacking-and-nude-celebrity-photos/?sh=3f8725462de7

Jane Armstrong, "Say 'cheese," *The Globe and Mail*, December 2003; https://www.theglobeandmail.com/news/national/say-cheese/article20452950/

"Pic of Naked Canadian Mayor Stolen from Computer," *Associated Press* via *SFGATE*, December 11, 2003; https://www.sfgate.com/politics/article/Pic-Of-Naked-Canadian-Mayor-Stolen-From-Computer-2508931.php

## CHAPTER 3: PICTURES AND POSTS YOU CAN CONTROL

Lauren Salm, "70% of employers are snooping candidates' social media profiles," Careerbuilder.com, June 15, 2017; https://www.careerbuilder.com/advice/social-media-survey-2017

"Is Facebook Evidence Admissible in a Court of Law," Page-Vault.com, November 15, 2019; https://www.page-vault.com/resources/is-facebook-evidence-admissible-in-a-court-of-law/

Twitter, thread on #barabooproud: https://twitter.com/jules_su/status/1061863594885824512

Emily Sullivan, "Photo Of Students Giving Nazi Salute Being Investigated By Wis. School District," NPR, November 13, 2018; https://www.npr.org/2018/11/13/667288781/photo-of-students-giving-nazi-salute-being-investigated-by-wisc-school-district

Christina Caron, "Students Who Made Apparent Nazi Salute in Photo Won't be Punished," *New York Times*, November 11, 2018; https://www.nytimes.com/2018/11/24/us/baraboo-wisconsin-nazi-salute-photo.html

Chris McGreal, "The Nazi salute picture that divided an American town," *The Guardian*, January 10, 2019; https://www.theguardian.com/us-news/2019/jan/10/nazi-salute-picture-baraboo-wisconsin-divided-american-town

Catherine Bosley interview with Katelyn Bowden, Image Abuse Victim Advocate, Founder B.A.D.A.S.S. Army, November 10, 2017; https://badassarmy.org/

Lucia Graves, "A topless photo ruined this teacher's career. Now she's speaking out," *The Guardian*, April 19, 2019; https://www.theguardian.com/lifeandstyle/2019/apr/19/lauren-miranda-teacher-topless-photo-speaks-out

Amanda Lenhart and Maeve Duggan, "Couples, the Internet, and Social Media," Pew Research Center, February 11, 2014; https://www.pewresearch.org/internet/2014/02/11/couples-the-internet-and-social-media/

Sheri Madigan, PhD, Anh Ly, MA, Christina L. Rash, BA, "Prevalence of Multiple Forms of Sexting Behavior Among Youth," *JAMA*, April 2018; https://jamanetwork.com/journals/jamapediatrics/fullarticle/2673719

Caitlin Dewey, "A guide to safe sexting: How to send nude photos without ruining your life, career and reputation," *Washington Post*, July 11, 2014; https://www.washingtonpost.com/news/the-intersect/wp/2014/07/11/a-guide-to-safe-sexting-how-to-send-nude-photos-without-ruining-your-life-career-and-reputation/

Catherine Bosley, "Declaring War on Revenge Porn," *Ms. Magazine*, January 19, 2018; https://msmagazine.com/2018/01/19/declaring-war-revenge-porn/

Cyberbullying.org, "Sexting Laws Across America," https://cyberbullying.org/sexting-laws

## CHAPTER 4: PICTURES AND POSTS YOU CANNOT CONTROL

"Yolanda," "How Many Times Are You Caught on Security Camera per Day," *Reolink*, October 19, 2018, by https://reolink.com/how-many-times-you-caught-on-camera-per-day/

Catherine Bosley interview with Timothy Dimoff, Founder/Director Sacs Consulting and Investigative Services, Inc., Akron, Ohio; November 27, 2017; sacsconsulting.com

## CHAPTER 5: YOUR WRITTEN WORDS

Jon Ronson, "How One Stupid Tweet Blew Up Justine Sacco's Life," February 2, 2015, *New York Times*, https://www.nytimes.com/2015/02/15/magazine/how-one-stupid-tweet-ruined-justine-saccos-life.html

Jon Ronson, *So You've Been Publicly Shamed*, March 2016, Riverhead Books, pages: 70, 72-73

## CHAPTER 6: ONLINE SHAMING OR BULLYING

Lindsay Dodgson, "A psychotherapist says there are four types of shame—here's what they are and how they affect us," *Business Insider*, April 3, 2018; https://www.businessinsider.com/different-types-of-shame-2018-3

Michelle Miller, "Bullies use social media to urge 12 year old to kill herself," CBS News, September 16, 2013; https://www.cbsnews.com/news/bullies-use-social-media-to-urge-12-year-old-to-kill-herself/

Kelly Wallace, "Police file raises questions about bullying in Rebecca Sedwick's suicide," CNN.com, April 21, 2021; https://www.cnn.com/2014/04/18/living/rebecca-sedwick-bullying-suicide-follow-parents

Matt Gutman and Josh Haskell, "Rebecca Sedwick Suicide: Parents of Alleged Cyberbully Blame Facebook Hack," ABC News, October 16, 2013; https://abcnews.go.com/US/parents-alleged-rebecca-sedwick-cyberbully-blame-facebook-hack/story?id=20583537

Elisha Fieldstadt, "She should be here: Two Girls Charged in Case of Florida Bullied Girl Who Committed Suicide," NBC News, October 15, 2013; https://www.nbcnews.com/news/us-news/she-should-be-here-two-girls-charged-case-bullied-florida-flna8C11397670

Catherine Bosley interview with Michael Shelby, Founder/Director: Technology Addiction Center, Hartford, CT; January 22, 2021, https://technologyaddictioncenter.com/about/

## CHAPTER 7: THE GOOD NEWS: YOU CAN RESCUE YOUR REPUTATION

Catherine Bosley interview with Aaron Gervais, Head of Strategic Communications, ReputationDefender.com, March 26, 2020; https://www.reputationdefender.com/

Maeve Duggan, Pew Research Center, "Online Harassment," Pew Research Center, October 22, 2014; https://www.pewresearch.org/internet/2014/10/22/online-harassment/

Marie Ennis-O'Connor, "How To Handle Social Media Trolls," *Health Care Social Media*, July 31, 2018, hcsmmonitor.com, https://hcsmmonitor.com/2018/07/31/how-should-you-handle-social-media-trolls/

Catherine Bosley interview with Michael Shelby, Founder/Director: Technology Addiction Center, Hartford, CT; January 21, 2021; https://technologyaddictioncenter.com/about/

Carson King, apology, Twitter, September 24, 2019; Carson King on Twitter: https://t.co/5pM1D6jh5H/ Twitter

Laura Laughead, "College football fan to donate over $157,000 to hospital after viral 'beer money' plea," ABC News, GMA, September 20, 2019; https://abcnews.go.com/GMA/Living/college-football-fan-donate-40000-hospital-viral-beer/story?id=65689221

Aaron Calvin, "Meet Carson King, the Iowa Legend who's raised more than $1 million for charity off a sign asking for beer money," *The Des Moines Register*, September 24, 2019; https://www.desmoinesregister.com/story/sports/college/iowa-state/football/2019/09/24/meet-carson-king-whos-raised-over-1-million-charity-asking-beer-money-childrens-hospital-tweet/2427538001/

Kat Tenbarge, "A reporter who dug up a local hero's old offensive tweets was fired for his own offensive tweets," *Insider*, September 29, 2019; https://www.insider.com/des-moines-regis-ter-aaron-calvin-fired-carson-king-offensive-tweets-2019-9

Katie Shepherd, "Iowa reporter who found a viral star's racist tweets slammed when critics find his own offensive posts," *Washington Post*, September 26, 2019; https://www.washington-post.com/nation/2019/09/25/carson-king-viral-busch-light-star-old-iowa-reporter-tweets/

Geneseo Brewing supports Carson King, Facebook.com, September 25, 2019; https://www.facebook.com/Geneseo-Brewing/photos/a.1520372228215262/2342141159371694/?-type=3&theater

Carson King's Foundation Website: https://carsonkingfoun-dation.org/

## CHAPTER 8: PACT PAST IT

Ryu Takizawa, M.D., Ph.D., Barbara Maughan, Ph.D., and Louise Arseneault, Ph.D., "Adult Health Outcomes of Childhood Bullying Victimization: Evidence from a Five-Decade Longitudinal British Birth Cohort," *The American Journal of Psychiatry*, July 1, 2014; https://ajp.psychiatryonline.org/doi/10.1176/appi.ajp.2014.13101401

Ainoa Mateu, Pascual-Sánchez, Maria Martinez-Herves, Nicole Hickey, Dasha Nicholls, Tami Kramer, "Cyberbullying and post-traumatic stress symptoms in UK adolescents," *BMJ Journals: Archives of Disease in Childhood*, September 18, 2020; https://adc.bmj.com/content/105/10/951.info

Sue Scheff, "Adult Cyberbullying Is More Common Than You Think," *Psychology Today*, November 29, 2019; https://www.psychologytoday.com/us/blog/shame-nation/201911/adult-cyberbullying-is-more-common-you-think

Meng-Jie Wang, Kumar Yogeeswaran, Nadia P. Andrews, Diala R. Hawi, Chris G. Sibley, "How Common Is Cyberbullying Among Adults? Exploring Gender, Ethnic, and Age Differences in the Prevalence of Cyberbullying," *Mary Ann Liebert, Inc. Publishers*, November 7, 2019; https://www.liebertpub.com/doi/10.1089/cyber.2019.0146

Maeve Duggan, "Online Harassment 2017," Pew Research Center, *Internet & Technology*, July 11, 2017; https://www.pewresearch.org/internet/2017/07/11/online-harassment-2017/

Barton Goldsmith, Ph.D., "Don't Bury Your Feelings. Being in touch with your emotions will make you a better person," *Psychology Today*, November 4, 2013; https://www.psychologytoday.com/us/blog/emotional-fitness/201311/dont-bury-your-feelings\

Catherine Bosley interview with Dr. Tamar Blank, PsyD., Founder/Director Riverdale Psychology, Riverdale, NY, January 26, 2021; https://www.riverdalepsychology.com/copy-of-our-team

Beth Dalbey, "Understanding The Bully: They're Often Victims, Too, Experts Say," *Patch*, October 22, 2018; https://patch.com/us/across-america/bully-menace-experts-understanding-bully

Sherri Gordon, "8 Motives Behind Why Kids Cyberbully," *Very Well Family*, July 11, 2020; https://www.verywellfamily.com/reasons-why-kids-cyberbully-others-460553

Sue Scheff, "Finding Online Support for Cyberbullying and Shaming," *Huffpost,* October 13, 2017; https://www.huffpost.com/entry/finding-online-support-for-cyberbullying-and-shaming_b_59dfc240e4b09e31db975775

Aad Boot, "This too shall pass, said Lincoln, and What it Means for Leadership Today," *Leadership Watch*, September 21, 2019; https://leadershipwatch-aadboot.com/2019/09/21/this-too-shall-pass-said-lincoln-and-what-it-means-for-leadership-today/

# INTERVIEWS

Catherine Bosley interview with Richard Storrs, Attorney, The Storrs Law Firm, Atlanta, GA, March 30, 2020; https://www.storrslaw.com/attorneys/richard-storrs/

Catherine Bosley interview with Katelyn Bowden, Image Abuse Victim Advocate, Founder B.A.D.A.S.S. Army, November 10, 2017; https://badassarmy.org/

Catherine Bosley interview with Timothy Dimoff, Founder/Director Sacs Consulting and Investigative Services, Inc., Akron, Ohio; November 27, 2017; sacsconsulting.com

Catherine Bosley interview with Michael Shelby, Founder/
Director: Technology Addiction Center, Hartford, CT; January
22, 2021; https://technologyaddictioncenter.com/about/

Adam Petrilli, May 2022, CEO/Founder of
NetReputation.com; https://www.netreputation.com/

Catherine Bosley interview with Dr. Tamar Blank, PsyD.,
Founder/Director Riverdale Psychology, Riverdale, NY,
January 26, 2021; https://www.riverdalepsychology.com/copy-
of-our-team

# RESOURCES FOR YOU

Catherine Bosley, "My Naked Nightmare: A Lesson in Surviving Humiliation," TEDx Talk, December 2018; https://www.ted.com/talks/catherine_bosley_my_naked_nightmare_a_lesson_in_surviving_humiliation

BADASS ARMY: https://badassarmy.org/

Cyberbullying.org, "Sexting Laws Across America," https://cyberbullying.org/sexting-laws

Cyberbullying.org, "Cyberbulling Stories," https://cyberbullying.org/stories

Heartmob, https://iheartmob.org/

Sue Scheff, "Finding Online Support for Cyberbullying and Shaming," Huffpost, October 13, 2017; https://www.huffpost.com/entry/finding-online-support-for-cyberbullying-and-shaming_b_59dfc240e4b09e31db975775
https://www.stompoutbullying.org/bullying-cyberbullying-crime

Carson King Foundation: https://carsonkingfoundation.org/

"Facebook Fired: Legal Standards for Social Media Based Terminations of K-12 Public School Teachers," Sage Open, March 12, 2015, by Kimberly W. O'Connor, Gordon B. Schmidt; https://journals.sagepub.com/doi/full/10.1177/2158244015575636

www.ingramcontent.com/pod-product-compliance
Lightning Source LLC
Chambersburg PA
CBHW060532130626
46553CB00002B/722